A New Heart and a New Spirit

A Plan for Renewing Your Church

David S. Young

Judson Press ® Valley Forge

© 1994

Judson Press, Valley Forge, PA 19482-0851

Unless otherwise noted, Scripture quotations are from the Revised Standard Version of the Bible, copyright © 1946, 1952, 1971, by the Division of Christian Education of the National Council of the Churches of Christ in the U.S.A. Used by permission. Other Scripture quotations are from the NEW REVISED STAND-ARD VERSION of the Bible, copyrighted 1989 by the Division of Christian Education of the National Council of the Churches of Christ in the United States of America, and are used by permission (NRSV). The *Good News Bible*, copyright © American Bible Society, 1976. Used by permission (GNB).

Library of Congress Cataloging-in-Publication Data
Young, David S. (David Samuel), 1944-
   A new heart and a new spirit : a plan for renewing your church / David S. Young.
      p.   cm.
   Includes bibliographical references.
   ISBN 0-8170-1209-5
   1. Church renewal. I. Title.
   BV600.2.Y68 1994
262'.001' 7—dc2094-17186

Printed in the U.S.A.

94 95 96 97 98 99 00 01 02 03   10 9 8 7 6 5 4 3 2 1

A New Heart and a New Spirit

A Plan for Renewing Your Church

Table of Contents

Foreword vii

Acknowledgments ix

Introduction xi

The Steps Toward Renewal xvii

Chapter l: A Vision for Church Renewal 1
  Righting Our Approach 2
  Removing the Grave Cloths 2
  Finding a First-Person Faith 3
  Unbinding for Life 5

Chapter 2: Organizing for Church Renewal 7
  Identifying Strengths 8
  Discovering Identity 10
  Leading for Renewal 14
  Growing in Faith 17

Chapter 3: Planning for Church Renewal 21
  Envisioning Renewal 21
  Matching Needs and Strengths 25
  Setting Goals 28
  Establishing a Plan of Renewal 30

Chapter 4: Implementing the Plan of Renewal 35
  Setting Up a Ministry 35
  Enlisting 38
  Training 40
  Starting the Ministry 43

Chapter 5: Supervising Persons in Renewal 45
  Supervision 45
  Listening 46
  Identifying Growth Areas 48

Asking Permission 49
Discussing Resources 50
Developing an Action Plan 51
Modeling 52
Growing Spiritually 53

Chapter 6: Covenanting for Renewal 57
Encouraging Renewal 57
Understanding Growth 60
Assimilating New Members 64
Renewing and Serving 66

Chapter 7: The Church in Transformation 69
Creating a New Heart and a New Spirit 69
Renewal in the Churches 72
Mayfair Conwell 72
Calvary Baptist 76
Upland Baptist 79

Chapter 8: The Path to Joy 85
A Personal Pilgrimage of Faith 85
Openness As a Congregation 86
Confidence and Motivation 88
A Nurturing Community 90
A Worshiping Congregation 92
A Witnessing and Serving Church 94
Joy 96

Notes 99

Bibliography 105

Additional Places to Turn 107

Foreword

Renewal, both individual and corporate, is or should be a continuing concern of every congregation. David Young provides a useful resource for churches that are ready to address this universal need in a wholistic, systematic, and persistent way.

Too many churches have been snared by the plausible argument that they must "get their own house in order" before they can think of reaching out to others beyond their own church walls. Renewal is most likely to take place when those inside the walls are concerned about those outside the walls of the church. Therefore, mission and renewal are conducive to, but not contingent on, each other. That, however, is the paradoxical dilemma, for to be concerned about those outside their walls, church members must already have experienced some degree of renewal. Just as the desire to be faithful presupposes a degree of faith, so the desire for renewal is itself evidence of renewal. And just as the possibility of salvation is incipient in the very awareness of our need of salvation, so the possibility of church renewal is implicit in the church's awareness of its need of renewal.

A New Heart and a New Spirit is exactly what it purports to be: a plan for renewing your church. Pastors and lay leaders with a degree of spiritual commitment sufficient to seek the broad-scale renewal of the church will find this handbook a helpful guide. Drawing on his own experience in the parish and classroom, as well as the experience of the congregations that have participated in the church renewal process he has developed, the author lays out his vision for congregational renewal and offers some practical ideas and examples for organizing, planning, and implementing a thoroughgoing renewal process.

Dr. Young is aware of the acute need for ongoing discipling, and his chapter on supervising persons in renewal aptly addresses this concern. Just as discipling requires the mentor's commitment to "being with" the learner, so does Dr. Young's program call for an extensive and well-structured period of supervision. In addition, his emphasis on the importance of listening and of "modeling" is highly commendable; it is also totally compatible with the incarnational style of interpersonal witnessing I have long advocated and tried to represent in the approach that has come to be known as "service evangelism."

He also rightly stresses the need for "servant leadership," a popular expression designating a leadership style that is biblically and theologically conformable to the teachings and example of Jesus. Although Dr. Young's focus is on renewal and not on leadership development per se, he offers helpful ideas and suggestions on the role, the importance, and the style of leadership in the renewal process.

Dr. Young recognizes that renewal is an ongoing process, not an emergency operation to rescue a congregation that is foundering in the spiritual doldrums. The goal is not to win back inactive members but to keep them from becoming inactive in the first place. New members must also be assimilated, and Dr. Young's plan of renewal stresses the importance of intentionally fulfilling that obligation. Otherwise, too many folks will be slipping out the back door as fast as the church can bring them in the front door. A church needs an effective backdoor policy (assimilation) along with a successful front-door policy (outreach and evangelism) in order to avoid becoming just another revolving door.

A New Heart and a New Spirit is a healthy blend of general principles and practical suggestions. The author chooses as the biblical metaphor for his approach to church renewal the story of the raising of Lazarus from the dead and applies the image of unbinding to the broader concept of church renewal. Other biblical references serve further to punctuate, illustrate, and validate some of the author's key points. At a time when the far too prevalent tendency is to measure the "success" of a church in terms of its numerical growth rather than its spiritual faithfulness, Dr. Young has provided a much-needed corrective. His focus is on church renewal, not on church growth—although it is almost inevitable that any congregation that experiences genuine renewal will grow numerically as well as spiritually.

The *goal* of renewal, however, is not numerical growth. The goal of renewal is faithful, obedient discipleship. In that sense, renewal is a process in which individuals and churches should be continually involved. It is not a means to an end but an end in itself. Hats off to David Young for providing a programmatic way to achieve that end!

Richard Stoll Armstrong
Ashenfelter Professor Emeritus of Ministry and Evangelism
Princeton Theological Seminary

Acknowledgments

As a young pastor just out of seminary, I became very aware of the need for church renewal. This need—this yearning—exists not only for pastors but also for many persons in congregations. This handbook grew out of my initial longing to put together a helpful resource for renewal for pastors and laypersons. My intentions were formalized as the Bush Creek Church of the Brethren in Monrovia, Maryland, joined with me as part of a new Doctor of Ministry program at Bethany Theological Seminary. As the youngest pastor in that first class, I began to learn how a pastor and local church can enter a renewal process.

I wish to thank the seminary that instituted the program and the congregational supervisory group of that congregation, which helped guide the process. I also wish to express appreciation to my faculty advisory group from the seminary, as well as my peer advisory group in the Mid-Atlantic District, for their counsel. Their supervision kept the focus on church renewal in the plan of ministry.

I also want to express my gratitude to other congregations in which the renewal process became real. Included in that process are the churches of four different denominations that participated in the Transformational Sunday School Project of the Atlantic Northeast District of the Church of the Brethren. The findings of that study helped inform and confirm the process of renewal. My liberal use of examples in this resource draws heavily on the learnings of dedicated people in a variety of church settings.

I wish to express appreciation to the students of the Eastern Baptist Theological Seminary in Philadelphia, Pennsylvania, whose input and enthusiasm for the classes on church renewal that I teach have continually challenged my thinking. Three examples of churches that engaged in the process of renewal taught in those ongoing classes are included in this resource. Each pastor and church is offered my heartfelt support and gratitude.

I would like to extend a special thanks to Dr. Manfred Brauch, president of Eastern Baptist Theological Seminary, who, upon seeing the response to the church renewal courses, encouraged me to go to Princeton Theological Seminary. There Dr. Richard Stoll Armstrong, Ashenfelter Professor of Ministry and Evangelism, graciously received me into a mentoring program where these thoughts could be further developed into written form. Richard has truly been a mentor, colleague, and friend. Harold Rast, Kristy Arnesen Pullen, Mary Nicol, Patricia Finn, and Tina Edginton of Judson Press lent their invaluable assistance to the manuscript's development, and editor Kathleen Hayes did an excellent job of refining, shaping, and enhancing the manuscript into its final form.

One other very important team has provided invaluable help—my family. My sons, Jonathan and Andrew, have provided their help from suggestions on title and opening to computer assistance and unbounding enthusiasm. My wife, Joan, has given invaluable support, helping by many readings of the text and by encouraging that the resource be practical. Integral to this team has been the presence of the One from whom new life springs forth. This resource could not have been developed without the divine help that has made this resource a joyful reality.

Introduction

"Get ready for church renewal!" So began the breakfast conversation as my family gathered for waffles and talked about the opening words of this book. Soon the conversation turned to RAM and ROM, Hamming codes and hard-disc drives, as the engineering students around the table began talking computers.

I had to think, What does this have to say about church renewal? But then I reflected further. How often when we talk about church renewal, I thought, do we hear language that is strange to us or concepts that seem inconsistent with our understanding of faith? Moreover, we may feel we do not have the human resources or the high quality of effective leadership to facilitate renewal. As with the computer language, we may feel all of this is beyond not only our understanding but our application.

So how do we get ready for church renewal?

A New Heart and a New Spirit is a practical handbook for preparing you for and guiding you in the process of church renewal. Its content grew out of my experiences as a pastor in the local church. Affirming the power of the gospel message, this program begins where we are and builds a practical way to enable renewal in the church. Leadership will be developed, and strengths of the congregation will be affirmed. Spiritual depth will be explored, and a plan of renewal will be developed. Further, we will explore how to implement that plan, which will entail not only training leaders but supervising individuals as they grow in their ministries. A vital part of this process will be to explore how spiritual growth is intertwined with renewal in the church.

I offer examples throughout this handbook to illustrate this growth and renewal process, beginning with a project of church renewal at Bush Creek Church of the Brethren in Monrovia, Maryland, which was the basis of a Doctor of Ministry program, and then expanding to include other churches where renewal is occurring. We will witness the spiritual progress of three churches actually involved in the process suggested in this book. As you observe these three churches, you may find yourself relating to their struggles and process. Whatever your situation, this resource is designed to begin where you are in your church and help you discover God's gift of a new heart and a new spirit.

The first congregation we will meet is Mayfair Conwell Memorial Baptist Church, located in a residential Caucasian neighborhood in Northeast Philadelphia. It is an American Baptist congregation of approximately 150 members, 90 percent of whom reside in the Philadelphia area. The congregation is made up of three primary extended-family units, with many relational ties among the members. The worshiping community averages eighty per week and is made up of some young families plus a significant population of older adults. The church is fifty-eight years old and is comprised mostly of "blue-collar" workers with a high school education. The church finds itself, along with Methodists, Presbyterians, Lutherans, and Episcopalians, sandwiched between two large Catholic parishes on either end of the neighborhood. Also characteristic of this changing community is the lack of new employment opportunities.

Rev. Marcia Bailey was serving the congregation as pastor when she enrolled in the course on church renewal I teach at Eastern Baptist Theological Seminary. In identifying the need for renewal, Marcia noted that the aging population of this congregation, along with its static membership figures and the pending burnout of its handful of core leaders, made it clear that it was ripe for renewal. Along with all this, Rev. Bailey sensed that this congregation had conditioned itself to accept what she would call a "survival motif." Knowing they were small and aging, they were resigned to think of themselves as "just hanging on," even though they had many positive qualities and a real depth of faith. Marcia envisioned a sense of confidence for them, a self-assuredness that would be invigorating for the congregation and inviting to the community.

The second congregation is Calvary Baptist Church, a historic African American church situated in Chester, Pennsylvania. Chester is a small urban community of approximately forty-five thousand people located in the corridor between Philadelphia, Pennsylvania, and Wilmington, Delaware; 65 percent of its population is African American. As home to several major companies, including Penn Ship, Sun Ship, Reynolds Aluminum, and Ford, it was an industrial boomtown through much of this century until the seventies and early eighties, when many of the businesses shut down or relocated. Now, Chester hosts mostly smaller employers in service industries and deals with the typical inner-city problems of urban America.

Historically, Calvary Baptist was at the forefront of all movements in Chester. Calvary was in the vanguard denominationally as its most long-serving pastor, Dr. J. Pius Barbour, served as editor for the *National*

Baptist Voice magazine. Calvary nurtured many well-known Baptist leaders—including Dr. Martin Luther King, Jr.; Dr. Samuel Proctor; Dr. W. S. Jones, Jr.; and Dr. Harold Carter—during their days of matriculation at Crozer Theological Seminary, which until 1970 was located in Chester/Upland. The church consists of several extended families from Chester. However, several new families from Chester and the adjoining tri-state area now make up the congregation.

What led the pastor, Rev. Tommy Jackson, to feel a need for renewal was the lack of vision for what the church could become. He knew the church needed to develop an expanded leadership in order to give congregants a greater sense of ownership. As pastor, Tommy also noted a personal need for renewal; he questioned whether his leadership style was too dogmatic, independent, exclusive, and singular. He wanted to seek God's guidance to "lead me through the process and development of a plan that would be inclusive of and acceptable to the church leadership." Any plan, he knew, had to be "ours not mine." He was ready to envision more for himself and his church in this Chester community—a renewed love for Christ, the church, and the world.

The third congregation stands at the crossroads between this troubled urban area and middle-class suburbia. The Upland Baptist Church is a congregation with an average weekly worship attendance of slightly over 150 people. The church has a strong central core of members who minister to the larger church membership, which "on paper" is five hundred plus. This core of faithful membership also has a strong sense of mission to the Upland community, a small historic town of about thirty-three hundred residents. The church has been influenced by long pastorates; the former pastor served for thirty-seven years, and the current pastor, Rev. Dale Miller, is nearing his fourteenth year of ministry. Due to the long tenures and the nature of the church's mission, the pastor often takes on the role of a kind of town chaplain, providing ministry to families and helping with community projects. Besides the regular program of study, worship, prayer, and fellowship, Upland Baptist has a weekly food-bank ministry that provides emergency assistance to forty to fifty families. Every Friday evening, seventy-five young people between ages four and eleven may be found at the church watching movies and playing games as part of the Upland Baptist Children's Theater. Most ministries of the church have an intentional service or mission emphasis.

The church's need for renewal stems in part from trying to respond to the needs of the transitional community out of God's call to ministry. The pastor states, "As our church goes through various transitions and the communities around us continue to be in what seems a state of chaotic change, we sense that the church needs a new heart and a new spirit to meet the new demands of Christ in our day." The need for renewal also takes on a personal meaning for Dale. "Personally, after fourteen years of ministry in one place, I have sensed a need for spiritual renewal, for something creatively new to excite me in ministry. I have longed to be part of a congregation that is not only 'busy' but spiritually alive in the process of the many things we are and do for our Lord. While I have enjoyed a deep Christian friendship with many in the congregation and feel loved and supported, I have often craved a deeper spiritual reality. In the context of church ministry, this cannot happen in isolation. I find myself in search of a community of faith that is renewed and alive."

This need for renewal is felt by others in the congregation. The faithful saints who regularly support the ministries of a church with time and stewardship can grow weary. "Without these seasons of renewal, the church will burn itself out, and our spiritual resources for ministry will diminish," says Dale. Moreover, if the church is going to draw new people to the fellowship, they must have something to offer that is alive and invigorating. People in our society are often broken by the strains and stresses of life; they will not often go to a church that is not alive and upholding a strong sense of mission. "If we are going to invite new people to come or keep the many who visit," Dale surmises, "we must be 'living saints' and a renewed community. For these reasons renewal is seen as more than a programmatic goal. It is necessary to have at the core of who we are for Christ the energy of his Spirit that empowers our mission."

This book outlines an intentional process of growth in three major phases: organizing, planning, and implementing. It suggests forming a special renewal committee with a broad-based membership, and the pastor (or pastors) working as a team with the committee to move through the stages of renewal. If such a group already exists, it would be natural to call on them to fulfill such responsibilities. Strong leadership will be needed if the process is to work. We will also see how the cycles of organizing, planning, and implementing will recur as new arenas of ministry are discovered.

In considering the organizational stage, we will look at how to determine the strengths of a congregation. What is unique about this church and its people? Next we will look at the biblical call for renewal. What biblical images tug at us? What is our mandate? We will also consider a unique servant leadership style to fulfill a diverse role of supervision and spiritual guidance. Then we will aim to discover a vision for a congregation. In the midst of needs for ministry, how can a congregation build a sense of positive identity? Matching needs with congregational strengths will be crucial.

In the planning phase, we will explore how to establish a three-year, intentional plan for renewal that is both practical and achievable. This will include envisioning renewal by using the servant leadership concept.

Out of this will arise working goals—concrete statements with concrete time frames—that are closely tied to matching needs and strengths. The plan of renewal is rooted in the local congregation and in concrete possibilities over a specified time.

In the implementing phase, as persons are called to ministry both in the church and in their individual lives, the need emerges for training and supervision for ministry. We will outline a training process that can be used in the local church and consider a seven-phase plan for supervision that will help persons implement their ministries. Next we'll look at covenanting for renewal, which helps the process of growth take more permanent shape. The inner dynamics of encouraging renewal, understanding growth, assimilating new members, and serving others will be topics of practical pursuit. Finally, we will look at the transformation of a church, including the results of the process in three very different churches.

Each section of this handbook follows a similar pattern for applying the steps toward renewal. We explore the background and rationale for each step of renewal, including the theory behind what we are doing, and then highlight each step of the renewal process and follow it with a plan for implementation. Each section concludes by looking at outcomes because this entire handbook is intended to be outcome-oriented, first building on our biblical call and then implementing each step of renewal. While renewal is never a simple linear process, these suggestions can facilitate a church's own pilgrimage. Add, adapt, and rearrange these suggestions according to the unique needs and strengths of your own congregation.

So how do we get ready for church renewal? How do we grow in spiritual depth while at the same time reaching out in service? With all the dreams and visions we might have for renewal, where do we begin? What do we mean by "renewal" anyway? Is this just another packaged plan to impose on a congregation? What if we don't have the necessary resources or leaders?

These and other questions immediately face us. Seeing ourselves in the churches above, and having other conditions as well with which to cope, what can we do? This entire resource is designed to answer these very questions. By beginning with a biblical focus, we will plumb the Scriptures to find a calling to renewal. We will explore what to do to help renewal become an intentional process by building on this calling and by developing those unique strengths that are part of a congregation. This handbook outlines what to do.

The final outcomes are of God's making. As we will see in the closing chapters, the churches who went through their plans of renewal had entirely new ministries emerge—beyond what they'd ever planned. Spiritual growth meant that people reached out in new and exciting ways. A new heart and a new spirit are the gifts of God. As God uses our every effort to bring growth and transformation, more than the expected happens. As we will see in the first chapter, renewal calls for adjustments to a new life, but the sense of new life will confirm that God's presence is at work. The results are often beyond what we anticipated. Renewal is God's gift. God wills new life for the church. God wills vitality and joy!

So get ready for church renewal!

The Steps Toward Renewal

Step Toward Renewal #1 (p. 9)

Draw together as many congregants as possible to identify the strengths of the congregation and celebrate the unique life of the church.

Step Toward Renewal #2 (p. 12)

Take the list of strengths to the board or leadership team, determine the unique identity of the congregation, and call an ongoing renewal committee to develop a plan for church renewal.

Step Toward Renewal #3 (p. 15)

Hold an event for all church boards and committees that focuses on servant leadership and its effectiveness in proclaiming the gospel.

Step Toward Renewal #4 (p. 18)

Hold an event for all church boards and committees on how to nurture spiritual growth and make spiritual life central to all church efforts.

Step Toward Renewal #5 (p. 22)

Have the renewal committee spend a focused time in prayer, seeking a vision for the congregation that is built on its strengths and is faithful to God's calling.

Step Toward Renewal #6 (p. 26)

Have the renewal committee attempt, in light of its prayer and discernment, to match the congregation's needs with its strengths.

Step Toward Renewal #7 (p. 28)

Have a congregational goal-planning session in order to set realistic goals, determine concrete objectives by which to accomplish them, and establish a reasonable timetable.

Step Toward Renewal #8 (p. 30)

The committee establishes a plan of renewal to be in some way formalized with the entire congregation and dedicated at a Sunday morning worship service.

Step Toward Renewal #9 (p. 36)

Gather together the people who can make this ministry work by setting a course of action.

Step Toward Renewal #10 (p. 39)

Meet with persons invited to be part of the new ministry and build enthusiasm, share a calling, and enlist their help in clear and specific ways.

Step Toward Renewal #11 (p. 40)

The renewal committee establishes ongoing training to help persons grow in their ministries.

Step Toward Renewal #12 (p. 43)

After the planning and training process is complete, start the ministry.

Step Toward Renewal #13 (p. 46)

The renewal committee assigns a person to engage in a supervision process with the leader(s) of the new ministry.

Step Toward Renewal #14 (p. 58)

The renewal committee considers how to offset fears of renewal with encouragement and support and how to address any specific concerns.

Step Toward Renewal #15 (p. 62)

As a renewal committee, spend time assessing the congregation's points of growth and the vital balance of the components of church renewal.

Step Toward Renewal #16 (p. 64)

The renewal committee looks at the entire assimilation process and explores ways for persons to become part of the life of the congregation.

Step Toward Renewal #17 (p. 67)

The renewal committee gathers suggestions for meaningful service projects so that members can have options for making service a part of their journey of faith.

Chapter 1

A Vision for Church Renewal

How can new life—renewed life—come out of death? How can spiritual renewal be rediscovered in our personal lives and in the life of a church?

When a local church or national denomination has lost its cutting edge and is in decline, we naturally raise such necessary questions as these. At first, members may be defensive, denying the reality of the decline or attributing it to the church's pruning its roster. The whole church can actually be in denial, blocking out the fact that anything is really happening, that death is fast approaching. In its waning, the church often reflects the disillusionment and despair of the society of which it is a part.

As we look deeper, however, we discover that decline points us directly to issues of renewal. We can hear persons raise thought-provoking questions: What is the matter? Why is the church no longer a high priority in the lives of people? What hampers motivation? What accounts for the loss of leadership and the growing sense of apathy in the body of Christ? Why is our faith not more real? In its downturn, the church realizes that it can never exist on its prior commitments and usual programs, its prior faith and old vision. We remember that the biblical promise is one of hope, of vitality—yes, even of new life.

We desire a new heart and a new spirit, a deepened spiritual life. Long ago the prophet Ezekiel identified this human need. In his case, the nation of Judah was unresponsive to God and therefore fell into bondage in Babylonia. Enslaved to false loyalties, the nation of Judah had lost all life. Compromise was the hallmark of its people; violation of others was common. Unresponsive to God, the nation had formed a heart of stone (Ezekiel 11:19). Such deadness cuts across all time barriers, as apathy and loss of vision plague the church. At some point persons in a congregation realize they are in bondage. Helpless, they see they are victims of their circumstances, short-sighted vision, and inner division. At this stage, they become anxious to move from analysis to action, from despair to hope.

Fundamental change was needed among the people of Judah. Ezekiel envisioned for them "a new heart and a new spirit" (Ezekiel 11:19)—a hope that comes as God infuses new life. A new heart will pump vibrancy into the people; a new spirit is God's movement among them—healing, inspiring, and challenging. Ezekiel's call today is the call from within the church to find a new heart and a new spirit, to find renewal. We can affirm with Ezekiel that God reaches out as the shepherd and says, "They shall be my people, and I will be their God" (Ezekiel 11:20). As persons begin to discover a deep, abiding faith, they can discover that God is calling them to be a people with a new heart and a new spirit.

Righting Our Approach

We often mistakenly envision church renewal from the top down. Seeing the symptoms and outcome of a faltering church, the leaders decide on a plan. Like parents who see a faltering youth, they decide what is best and then establish expectations for action. The church council says what people should be doing and establishes a program for every conceivable need. The congregation sets goals, and the trustees upgrade the building. The executive committee hires adequate staff, while the social ministries committee sets up community programs. Yet low statistics indicate that something is still lacking. A positive experience must happen for people to come—and come back.

Even as we are laying out the best plans, low motivation drags down the dreams of the church. Fear of failure is often our most basic flaw. As leaders decide what others should do, they signal their frustration and anger and often give the impression of their own feelings of low self-worth and failure. Just consider how many negative messages are sent in one-liners in church newsletters to try to get people back to church. Indeed, can individuals grow in their sense of a spiritual life in this type of negative atmosphere?

Church renewal begins as persons feel the call of faith. It begins from the bottom up; it is not superimposed but rather is nurtured, guided, and sustained. If the church is to be renewed, individuals within it must have a clearer sense of purpose and mission. Renewal must begin with a whole new vision, a whole new orientation—a new heart and a new spirit!

Removing the Grave Cloths

The New Testament story of the raising of Lazarus (John 11:1-44) sets a good tone for our discussion of renewal within the church. In learning of the death of his good friend, Jesus takes his time before going to Bethany. As he arrives—four days after Lazarus's burial—he cuts through the attempts of Mary and Martha to blame him for not coming sooner, for letting the situation be as it is. How often in the face of death is someone present who is trying to blame someone! The view of Lazarus's family and friends is most dismal at this point; all they can see is death. In John's Gospel, however, the resurrection is already assumed. Jesus is risen, and new life *is* possible.

So often when we look at church renewal, we forget that its basis is the power of new life. We forget that the transformation of life, be it individual or corporate, happens within persons and within groups. In his dialogue with Martha about resurrection, Jesus speaks about this new life that occurs through transformation: "Whoever lives and believes in me shall never die." In response, Martha makes her great declaration: "Yes, Lord; I believe that you are the Christ, the Son of God, he who is coming into the world" (John 11:26-27). This transformation in faith is central to renewal.

The heart of new life in the church is people discovering their individual strengths and affirming their positive identity as a congregation. Finding a way to help them express and grow in their faith is the practical means to church renewal. As persons become clear in their purpose and find the training to respond to their callings, they become motivated for action. While painful at points, this process helps church members grow in maturity in the Christian life. As they encounter the limits, frustrations, and joys of practicing their faith, they mature in their sense of dependence on God. Spirituality develops as individuals grapple with enacting their calling. Out of death, new life comes forth.

In the story of the resurrection of Lazarus, we see how painful such growth can be for people. Objections are raised all around. Martha is aware of the odor of death—four days in the tomb. Have you ever been in a whole church that is dead? The atmosphere can be unpleasant—musty halls, broken furniture, bulletin boards filled with outdated notices. Worn-out staff maintain tattered yearbook directories of inactive members. Even the yellowed Easter lilies, donated in silk renditions, are too memorialized to be discarded. Precedents are strongly operative, and people turn to the past to determine what should happen in the present. Who dares speak of resurrection?

Finding a First-Person Faith

My wife is Russian, Polish, and Lithuanian. Her grandparents came from the "old country." Their migration through Eastern Europe led them ultimately to the United States of America. Her maternal grandparents transferred their culture to the new country; they spoke Lithuanian, ate Lithuanian food, and upheld the traditions of the old country. Even their appearance and manner revealed their heritage. This is particularly apparent at a family funeral, where the culture often appears in its purest form. The native language is spoken, and everyone assumes relatives know the old ways. The elders expect the faith of the old country to be present in the lives of the next generation. Bonded together as a community, they carry themselves forward as a group.

Much of the original culture is actually lost in the daily life of the second generation, however. The offspring speak of their parents' customs, and on special occasions they love to make dishes like borscht, kielbasa, and nut rolls. They may understand the language but cannot speak it, except for some lingering expressions. They smile as they speak of family members in the old country, but the experience of being Lithuanian is absent, and the old community is scattered. By the third generation, most of these remnants feel lost to us, and we attempt to connect to our roots by picking up a pierogi at a deli and thus participate somehow in being Lithuanian. The spirit, however, is gone.

Similarly, rather than being a third-generation hand-me-down, our faith must likewise be actively practiced to be an integral part of our lives. We must experience our beliefs in practice in our own lives. We sense a call; we feel the spirit of Christ. Our desire for renewal begins as we sense a purpose to our own personhood. For faith to be "first person," it must become an integral part of our mission, not just an empty weekly ritual. We must have a quiet assurance in our heart that the Spirit is alive and moving within us, that the kingdom is growing even in our own lives. We see the church also become stronger as first-person mission is discovered. The ministry discussed in this handbook is part of our daily lives as we come to experience our faith in the first person and live this faith as a dynamic life. As a result, ministry is transformed into action.

A church undergoing renewal consists of members who are actively engaged in their own pilgrimage of faith. Consultants of the Alban Institute conducted an intensive study of twelve growing churches in so-called mainline denominations. In their study, they identified a process that persons go through as they attend a new church. First, newcomers test the waters to see what the church is all about. They return only if the church has helped them on their own pilgrimage of faith. Affiliating with others and going deeper in their faith journey is crucial for persons to stay. The Alban researchers also discovered that a personal discipline of faith must be matched by some meaningful task in the church related to spiritual growth.[1] Newcomers must become authentically engaged for personal spiritual growth to occur, and they long for a faith pilgrimage that is "active in the first person."

Unbinding for Life

Could it be that our vision for personal spiritual growth and church renewal must begin with unbinding? As with Lazarus, the grave cloths that signify death and restrict life and growth must be removed. We must cast off old, accumulated notions of ministry by applying our renewed faith. Isn't it a step of faith—and outright risk—to remove grave cloths, the marks of death? Peeling off what is binding life is an awesome, if not fearful, task. But we must listen to and obey the Master. When we call him to the scene, listen to his words, and follow his instructions, we will discover our mission. Renewal begins with the resurrection becoming a personal reality in our daily lives, and growth occurs as we practice our faith.

Renewal is not only possible; it is God's will. In fact, in Christ resurrection—renewal—has already happened. Once we discover this new heart and new spirit, we will wonder why we ever settled for the old life. Although our growth will not be painless, we will discover a whole new spiritual depth emerging in the process of renewal. What can be more exciting than the promise of new life? What can be more thrilling than to see others growing beyond what one imagined was possible? By removing the grave cloths, we will know that the grace of Christ is sufficient for our every need and ahead of our every expectation. As we learn to apply our faith to all our life situations, our unbinding will give way to personal and corporate liberation; such a practice of faith should in turn make a tremendous impact on the society of which we are a part.

"Unbinding for life" is an intentional process of equipping, training, and supervising. People come alive in faith as they are given tools for growth. Some old patterns will need to be discarded as they find new life with new goals, new skills, and new inner purpose. Additional training and supervision will help that new growth become part of new life. In renewal we discover the power of Christ within, and when we claim that strength, then new power and priorities guide our hope. Unbinding for life is the opportunity for the church to affirm the gospel in all its power and promise. The living and incarnate Jesus will challenge our lethargy and overcome our death. As Jesus said to those who witnessed the resurrection of Lazarus, "Unbind him, and let him go."

Chapter 2

Organizing for Church Renewal

Believing by faith that renewal is possible, where do we begin? We may see so many weaknesses and failures in the church that we wonder how we are going to address them all. If we look at them in their totality, we can easily feel overwhelmed. In order to get beyond our paralysis, we must consider carefully where to start our process of church renewal.

After affirming the possibility of resurrection and new life, the next step is to identify our strengths rather than be overwhelmed by our weaknesses. Strengths are good indicators of where our talents lie; they are the promptings by which God may be calling us. Rather than focusing on its failures, a congregation can best begin its renewal by looking at its successes. This helps a congregation discover its identity and purpose.

In Chapter 1 we considered the biblical calling to new life in the church. In this chapter we will explore how to identify strengths, discover identity, and grow in faith. Church renewal proceeds as we take the church's biblical calling and match identified God-given strengths with evident needs (as we will discuss in detail in Chapter 3). The adjacent diagram best illustrates this interplay of forces and potential for growth. In the midst of this triangle of dynamic action, the creative work of spiritual growth and church renewal occurs. Organizing and planning for church renewal are two very important phases in the process and may take a year or more to complete, but it is important to ensure that this proper groundwork is in place for implementation to occur.

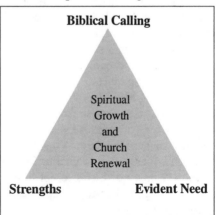

Biblical Calling

Spiritual Growth and Church Renewal

Strengths   Evident Need

Identifying Strengths

Background and Rationale

As we have indicated, the first step in church renewal is identifying the strengths of a congregation. The model of Jesus instructs us, for he was the Master of drawing forth new life. Jesus used each disciple's talents for the good of his whole ministry. For instance, Jesus built on Peter's boldness, on John's love, and on Andrew's quiet manner. Each was a unique person; each had a different task to accomplish; each played an integral role on the team.

Corporate renewal will begin as each member's potential is recognized and developed. As one career development book says, "To put it succinctly: Strengths *before* weaknesses. Or: Positive *before* negative."[1] In *What Color Is Your Parachute?* Richard Bolles suggests that career assessors look at the diaries of their lives in terms of their successes and identify the basic building blocks of their skills. They can then discover what they enjoy and what they do well.[2]

If this is true for individuals, it is certainly also true for congregations. In studying five successful Sunday schools, I found that this approach helped determine what factors made for "transformational experiences" for these congregations. Through visiting each church, I quickly learned that persons were eager to tell me what excited them. When I asked those in small groups to identify factors that were key to their success, over and over they said they built on their strengths. In fact, building on strengths stood out among the some twelve factors that actually led to their vitality. These churches gravitated toward their sources of energy, tapped these resources, and supported these efforts. Be it evening family-life gatherings, small-group shepherding programs, or after-school clubs meeting in renovated horse sheds, congregations built on their own individuality. They lived out of their God-given enthusiasm, power, and strength and demonstrated that "building on strengths means affirming who one is, feeling good about it, and yet striving for more."[3]

A congregation seeking renewal needs to identify what it has to offer its members and its community. "What makes us unique? What skills and talents has God given this church in order to do the work of the kingdom?" By identifying and celebrating its God-given uniqueness, a congregation can gain the courage to step out into new adventures of faith. The greater this awareness, the more persons will know what gifts they have and what they can share with others. A healthy sense of self-esteem as individuals and as a congregation is vital to faith formation. Remember: a year or more may be needed to accomplish the first four vital steps of renewal that are suggested in this chapter. But the results will be well worth waiting for!

Step Toward Renewal #1

Draw together as many congregants as possible to identify the strengths of the congregation and celebrate the unique life of the church.

This first step involves organizing a congregational event in which members gather in small groups in order to identify the positive experiences that have led to their own growth in faith. This event should be announced far in advance; consider having it take the place of the monthly business or committee meetings so that participants have the time to make the event a priority. Planners should use various formal and informal channels of communication to promote the event.

The pastor and official leadership team or executive committee may want to form what would be the beginning of an ongoing renewal committee to prepare for this meeting. Its structure can be lean at this point, although it has a very important job: to set up the congregational meeting—checking ahead and setting the best time, making up and mailing announcements, enlisting leadership and briefing persons on the event, and making as many follow-up phone calls as necessary to ensure that people will sense an enthusiasm and want to attend. Group leaders for the evening should be selected and briefed ahead of time on how to lead group discussion.

Keep the congregational gathering focused solely on renewal. After initial prayer and welcome, break the large group down into smaller groups and have the group leaders ask questions such as: "What is exciting to you about your faith? What experiences in this church community have changed your own life and encouraged your growth? What are your positive experiences in the church?" Two or three such questions should be enough to get the discussion and sharing started. Have the group leaders briefly summarize the experiences identified by group members on newsprint with magic marker. Usually the energy level rises during such an exercise, as participants are amazed at how many experiences they have had that have bolstered their faith and their appreciation of their church community. Be prepared for some moving, precious stories—and the possible shedding of some tears.

Next, have participants gather back together as a large group. Hang the listings of experiences for all to see. Highlight the common factors or elements that keep emerging, and discuss the strengths that are the common denominators of the total group experience. We can look behind the positive shared experiences and identify common elements in persons' experiences that made for growth in faith. Such factors may include love among people, special spiritual gifts, Bible study, leadership, and meeting needs of others.[4] These factors may be different for different people, but common elements will point not only to underlying themes that can lead to renewal but also to the unique identity of the congregation. The leader should compile this list on a separate piece of newsprint entitled "strengths of our church," to be taken back to the renewal committee for further study.

Close with celebration. For instance, have a litany of thanksgiving, lifting up what was shared item by item and having the group respond, "For this we give thanks." After some singing, prayers, and affirmations, have the group hold hands in a large circle and close with a hymn, such as "Blest Be the Tie That Binds." Serving refreshments afterwards will encourage folks to linger for more informal sharing; they may also offer one another support in the situations they face. This may be a unique experience for the church if members are unaccustomed to getting together to share their positive experiences of faith and how the church has helped them.

Outcomes

One of the outcomes of such an experience is that the energy level goes up. Persons begin to affirm the positive and share what has helped them grow in faith. They often hear for the first time what they mean to one another and the impact they have had on one another's lives. In effect, members claim what is unique to their church. This lays the foundation for building on past positive experiences and finding energy for renewal.

By identifying strengths, we move from a diagnostic model—finding out what's wrong and trying to fix it—to an affirming model—finding out what's right and building on it. In other words, the church begins to free itself from a pessimistic look-what's-wrong view and move towards a more positive here's-who-we-are outlook. In fact, persons can begin to experience the Good News firsthand and affirm that God *has* given new life—in special people; in talents that, when unleashed, can lead to satisfaction and growth; in the church's humble yet exciting mission. New life can emerge as individuals begin to identify their own sources of energy.

Another outcome is, of course, a concrete list of congregational strengths, which will serve as our building blocks for renewal. As the church begins to discover its calling and mission and affirms the strengths within its midst, it will discover and nurture a new heart and a new spirit.

Discovering Identity

Background and Rationale

By identifying strengths, a congregation begins to discover its identity. That identity is the corporate response to the calling of God. No congregation should attempt to copy what some other "successful" church is doing, for each congregation has its own unique gifts and potential. We need to ask of our own congregation, "What makes us special?"

One congregation I visited had such a diversity of people that I wondered what held them all together. As they shared the strengths and experiences that led to their growth in faith, however, I saw that they had learned to value one another. I also learned that they readily invited new people to participate in their services by reading a Scripture or offering a prayer. Newcomers did not have to be perfect or become members to offer their talents. This church had also developed an effective ministry to the disabled, meeting their needs and putting their gifts to use. As congregations like this one discover their purpose, they will see how persons can grow within the ministries that develop out of that purpose.

In its study of sixteen churches, the Alban Institute found that having a clear identity is vital to a congregation's growth:

"Members of growing churches think that they are special, unique, not like anyone else. They have a 'strength at the center,' a basic integrity or vigor at the center of parish life. In short, the congregation offers something of substance to people. That substance matches the basic human hunger within people seeking a church family. . . . The message the church proclaims is central to this identity. When it knows that its basic enterprise is to proclaim a message of faith, hope, and love to the world, and if it is doing it, it feeds its people with bread and not a stone. No amount of propaganda or organization will cover a lack of substance at the core."[5]

What Alban discovered was that while such churches did not necessarily have a good method of following up with new people, they did know who they were and where they were headed. Such an understanding of their identity attracted others.[6]

Another helpful way to understand a congregation's potential is to consider its size. Different-sized churches have different things to offer, and by understanding this, we can maximize the strengths of our particular church's size. In the excellent resource *Sizing Up a Congregation for New Member Ministry,* Arlin Rothauge looks at four sizes of churches and explores the natural strengths and identity of each. Family churches (up to 50 members) have a natural intimacy that is attractive. The pastoral church (50 to 150 members) offers contact with pastoral leadership that significantly shapes its life. The program church (150 to 350 active members) can offer a variety of programs to meet a broad range of needs. The corporate-sized church (350 to 500 or more members) has an aura that can be distinctive while smaller cell-groups help people feel included.[7]

Determining one's identity is a unique journey for a congregation. Too often churches are defeated by trying to be all things to all people or trying to be like other churches. For instance, how many church retreats are spent setting exciting and lofty goals, only to return home and find either that the congregation had false expectations or that their dreams were far from attainable? Instead, a congregation would be better off looking inward and discovering what factors have nurtured personal faith and energized the corporate church. Herein lie the clues to where God's call and human need meet. From here strengths become evident, mission emerges, and an identity is shaped.

Step Toward Renewal #2

Take the list of strengths to the board or leadership team, determine the unique identity of the congregation, and call an ongoing renewal committee to develop a plan for church renewal.

The board or leadership team should set aside an entire meeting to review the results of the congregational meeting and reflect on what makes the congregation special. The meeting should be a time of affirmation and appreciation as well as organizing. As the common threads identified at the congregational meeting are discussed, the unique identity of the congregation will become clear. If a number of people cite experiences from vacation Bible school or Sunday school or a church camp, the importance of Christian education will become evident. Perhaps experiences involving a particularly strong person who has nurtured many individuals or the role of many dedicated members will stand out. In one congregation, one person visited all the families of the kindergarten department. As a result, parents were eager to have their children in that class. Soon people were saying, "When I think of Christ Church, I think of that great kindergarten class."

After determining the congregation's unique strengths, the next step towards church renewal is to form a renewal committee to help the church shape and implement a three-year plan of renewal. The committee needs to be comprised of persons who have a real vision and commitment to Christ and the church. Consider not only those already in leadership positions but also those who have made a quiet impact on others and those who are enthusiastic and capable of helping spread the gifts they have been given. Another place to look for members of a renewal committee is among the newcomers. The renewal committee should have members who are involved in various areas of the life of the church. They should be freed in whatever ways possible to work on the three-year plan that lies ahead.

Initially such a group should spend time together praying and exploring their sense of God's call for the congregation as well the identity of the congregation set forth by the church leaders or board. They could spend additional time reviewing the strengths of the congregation and identifying the factors that have led to members' growth in faith.

It is also important for the committee to review some of the literature of church renewal listed at the end of this handbook and to contact its denomination's regional and national offices for additional resources on congregational renewal. The intent is not to build unrealistically high expectations for the church but to clearly identify those factors that will lead to transformation and new life. Such a review should help a renewal committee become more confident and focused. Remember: the starting point of renewal is to build on strengths. For this, understanding one's identity as a church is key.

Outcomes

By taking specific action, the congregation moves away from a state of helplessness and toward an attitude of thanksgiving. Leaders and congregants both begin to identify just what their congregation has to offer. They grow more aware of the various talents in their midst, and the source of their energy becomes more clear. The church also comes to realize its limitations and frees itself from lingering guilt over not having particular activities and programs that it used to have or the church down the street has. Being able to affirm what exists in the present helps a church become more open to what is possible in the future. A new heart and a new spirit begin to emerge.

The church thus begins to reflect a clearer understanding of its identity and a greater excitement for what it has to offer. Often individuals will put up announcements and posters that reflect their interests and beliefs. The building may begin to reflect new pride as worn areas are repainted and broken furniture is fixed. The newsletter begins to have fewer of those accusatory one-liners to prod people to action and more expressions of appreciation for what people have done. God helps us appreciate who we already are as well as what we can become.

While exciting, such changes can also be a bit scary. Is this just a temporary surge of energy? Will we be able to handle new things, new growth? Will we soon go back to the status quo? Persons may wonder where all this new excitement will lead; they may grow fearful of what they might have to give up.

Rather than seeing renewal as expanding and diversifying a congregation, we must first see renewal as centering and focusing.[8] New ministries may emerge, but they will grow naturally out of that which helps personal and corporate faith development. Nurturing a positive identity will require a positive leadership team to envision the future, encourage individuals, and guide church-wide renewal. Leadership is the catalyst for church renewal—and the topic to which we turn next.

Leading for Renewal

Background and Rationale

What type of leadership can turn the identifying of strengths into a practical program of renewal? Forget wishing for some magical individual with enough energy and drive to make everything just happen.[9] Forget wishing for an aptly trained high-tech manager who will provide a pleasing product and offer special coupons that fill the pews with people and keep the budget growing. That seems to work for the fast-food business, but for church renewal to occur, unlocking the energy required for transformation in the lives of people calls for an entirely different model of leadership.

The most suited style of leadership for church renewal is that of the servant leader. The servant leader is one who attempts to meet the needs of others. Servants take a basin and towel and wash the feet of those around them. The servant understands the power of demonstrating and living out the Christian gospel. The servant not only understands the way of Christ; the servant lives it. Such a leader's first concern is not to establish a program but to serve God and to serve the needs of other individuals and of the community at large. In servant leadership, trust and confidentiality grow because servants are not trying to pressure people or use them for their ends. Servants lift others up, helping them feel accepted and calling forth their strengths. Servant leadership releases energy for renewal.

Servanthood in ministry became real for me as I struggled to gain the perspective on church renewal that this handbook presents. Developing plans for ministry seemed to mean asking people to help initiate programs, and plans too often took precedence over people and became ends in themselves. A breakthrough came when I was able to see that programs were to serve people, and not vice versa. This freed me to see each moment as an opportunity to serve. A program can then follow, as servanthood gives purpose to planning. Servanthood is a posture to carry into ministry.[10] Servanthood begins with surrender and service to God, which leads us to learn the way of Christ. Servanthood leads to renewal.

Author Robert Greenleaf identifies the servant as leader—an idea he discovers in Hermann Hesse's *Journey to the East*.[11] In this make-believe journey, a band of men is accompanied by a servant named Leo, who does all the menial chores. The servant also sustains the group, however, "with his spirit and his song." Leo has what is described as an extraordinary presence, and when he disappears, the group falls apart and the journey is discontinued. Years later the narrator of the story, who had been on the journey, finds Leo and realizes that the servant was in fact the head of the group, "its guiding spirit, a great and noble leader."[12] The servant's role was in fact essential to the trip. For Greenleaf, the leader does not become a servant; rather the servant becomes a leader. Herein is the key to greatness in leadership: being a servant "deep down inside."[13]

Step Toward Renewal #3

Hold an event for all church boards and committees that focuses on servant leadership and its effectiveness in proclaiming the gospel.

In one class on leadership styles for church renewal, a layperson spoke enthusiastically about how his company, a major U.S. corporation, was doing the same thing we were talking about. Promoting servant leadership and meeting the needs of others, the company said, was an effective way to motivate people, to help them take initiative in their efforts and feel good about their labors. How much more so could a church have an event in which each church committee could look at leadership styles and their effects!

The best place to begin such exploration is the Bible, where ministry means servanthood. "Ministry" is the English translation of the Greek word *diakonia* or "service." The "ministry of reconciliation" Paul speaks about in 2 Corinthians 5:18 is the *"diakonia* of reconciliation." It is no surprise, then, that "early Christianity learned to regard and describe as *diakonia* all significant activity for the edification of the community . . ."[14] A crucial passage to look at is John 13:1-20, where Jesus washes the feet of the disciples. You might also read and discuss Mark 9:33-37, where Jesus teaches that "whoever wants to be first must be last of all and servant of all" (Mark 9:35). Servanthood describes the type of ministry done in Christ's name.[15] Other Scriptures on servanthood can lead us to new depths of understanding: being in the Father is emphasized in John 14:12-31; the manner and mission of the servant is described in the "suffering servant songs," such as Isaiah 42:1-4; servanthood as the way to Christlikeness and transformation is seen in Luke 22:24-27; and, as we will see in 1 Corinthians 8 (highlighted at the end of this book), servanthood even through hardship can bring joy. Such Scriptures and their implications for the church today could be studied, dramatized, and discussed in order to better understand how servanthood is the proper posture of the Christian life.

The monographs on servant leadership by previously mentioned author Robert Greenleaf are excellent, and I recommend that the group study them.[16] Several key components of the servant as leader speak directly to church renewal. The first is listening. In approaching a problem, Greenleaf points to the importance of listening first. Listening transforms people; listening builds strength in people.[17] It is crucial in renewal because when we approach problems with a listening ear, we begin to build a level of trust needed for renewal. Much of what is suggested in this resource, from identifying the strengths of a church to building a plan of ministry, will depend on good listening skills.

Acceptance and empathy are also important for servant leadership, according to Greenleaf. The servant is able to accept and value people as they are, while also seeing what they can become. In other words, we need to tolerate a certain amount of imperfection. For Greenleaf, the servant leader is able to lift a church or organization to a higher level. Servants have a special quality: they keep their ear close to the ground and therefore have the unique gift of foresight, which is the "central ethic of leadership."[18] Servants are able to feel patterns of growth. By listening closely enough to discover the strengths of a congregation, a servant leader can anticipate the components needed for a plan of renewal.

Finally, servant leaders have the gift of conceptualizing—what Greenleaf calls the "prime leadership talent."[19] Using the example of Danish folk high schools, Greenleaf analyzes what made this movement so strong. By nurturing the spirit of the common folk, Nikolai Frederik Severin Grundvig proposed a new form of education that used natural leaders and their own resources to train individuals in practical skills. Agricultural cooperatives were established, which brought about reform as the peasants emerged as a powerful force in society. As a result of Grundvig's leadership, this form of education had a major impact on Danish society.[20] Servant leaders are able to conceptualize what is possible and are therefore able to help people capture the spirit of what they can become. In church renewal, such leadership is vital not only for shaping what is possible but also for building step-by-step plans toward tangible goals.

On a local church level, after the church committees have studied the Scriptures and other resources on servant leadership, their conclusions could be shared at the next congregational meeting. People would sense that a major study in leadership has been done to help them in their ministry tasks. Throughout this resource, the concept of servant leadership will guide the way in shaping and implementing a plan of renewal and ongoing ministry.

Outcomes

A key to the energy needed for church renewal is this vital role of the servant leader. Like Jesus our model, the servant meets the needs of others and unlocks the energy of those in the group. Greenleaf put the test of the servant like this: "Do those served grow as persons; do they, while being served, become healthier, wiser, freer, more autonomous, more likely themselves to become servants?"[21] In other words, servants enable others to be servants. This dynamic interplay energizes, motivates, and facilitates renewal.

As a result, people begin to integrate their beliefs with their approaches in leadership. Often persons feel inadequate in leadership positions; they don't know where to begin, and they feel unsure of what the future requires. With the servant-leadership model, they can begin to anticipate what should be done next because they are mindful of the needs of others. They see the present beauty and possible growth; they begin where people are now and set step-by-step goals for what is possible for the future. Servant leaders effectively encourage the talents of others, and they see their own leadership as a ministry that enables others to grow in faith. Greenleaf concludes his monograph by pointing to the quality of the servant's inner life. Servant leaders begin their leadership from within, operating from the inside out.[22] That's why servant leadership is transformational by its very character and nature; it lifts others up and makes the journey feel possible. We can see what the servant role does, and that leads us back to the inner faith of such leadership.

In the next chapter, we will see how the servant-leader concept is crucial in establishing a plan of renewal in a congregation, for the servant leader facilitates the very wholeness of renewal.

Growing in Faith

Rationale and Background

Spiritual growth is nurtured by servant leaders and provides the energy for renewal. It doesn't happen in a vacuum; it happens as individuals feel the impact of the grace of God in their lives. That sense of inner strength prompts them to serve and encourage others. When persons begin to feel themselves growing in faith, they have a new energy, a new enthusiasm. In writing to the Romans, Paul shows his own high level of energy: "Through him God gave me the privilege of being an apostle, for the sake of Christ, in order to lead people of all nations to believe and obey" (Romans 1:5, GNB). He speaks of how persons begin to encourage one another in faith: "What I mean is that both you and I will be helped at the same time, you by my faith and I by your faith" (1:12, GNB). A new energy emerges as persons sense their mission and begin to encourage one another. Indeed, the quality of our inner life makes all the difference in the world—and is crucial for church renewal.

The process of church renewal is deeply intertwined with personal and corporate growth in faith. In the church, we can't just take an organizational model and expect it to bring renewal. The process of renewal must be attuned to what is called "spiritual direction." How are we growing in the process of mutual encouragement in faith? Are we attuned to the will of God? Do we sense that God's protective presence is allowing us to take creative risks? Are we growing and showing the fruits of the Spirit? What disciplines will help us rely more totally on the grace of God so that we have the strength to offer something to others? In short, how are we praying, sharing, and living the Good News?

This question may seem too obvious to ask, yet we can get so involved in maintaining the organization of the church that we forget the fundamental mission of the church. Christ is the only true resource for rejuvenating an otherwise burned-out congregation; he is the only One who provides the energizing, motivating force. This is *his* renewal project. The inner life of the church is fundamental in sustaining not only its own members but in feeding the deep hunger of those waiting to be drawn into its presence.

Step Toward Renewal #4

Hold an event for all church boards and committees on how to nurture spiritual growth and make spiritual life central to all church efforts.

Within most churches is some group responsible for overseeing the congregation's spiritual life. This may be the elders or the deacons or the pastoral board and staff. For renewal to begin, these persons should discuss what they hope to see in terms of spiritual nurture for the congregation. Initial discussion could consider how spiritual life is currently nurtured in the congregation. Next, explore what resources are available for those who want to grow in their spiritual lives. What reading materials are available, and to whom can one talk about spiritual concerns or about becoming a church member? What aids are available if a person wants to know more about their particular congregation? Each committee should consider how it can support the renewal effort. The renewal committee may want to meet with each committee and small group in the church. Everyone could benefit from becoming more aware of what is available for spiritual growth and discovering what has helped people grow.

In exploring factors that contributed to church growth, the Sunday school study mentioned earlier revealed that something was happening for adults in each church. They were intentionally attempting to grow in faith, and new adult classes were being established. When asked whether they felt their churches would continue to grow, one person answered, "I'm growing, and therefore we're growing." What a clear sense of rejuvenation and purpose![23] These churches considered themselves on intentional ventures of growth in faith. In order for a church to grow, persons must feel growth within themselves.

People grow best in their faith journey when they have others helping them along the way. This is true as individuals enter a church and as they take on ministries in the church or in their personal lives. While they are involved in ministry, they also need a place to explore their own growth and learn how to handle the practical situations they face in their lives. (See Chapter 5, "Supervising Persons in Renewal," for further discussion.) Feeling that personal growth is occurring helps offset burnout. This process of offering and seeking spiritual direction is re-energizing for persons who take up the call for renewal.

Outcomes

One outcome of such a focus is that personal faith becomes a more natural part of the church's life and conversation. Even business meetings will flow more easily as decisions are linked with personal and corporate faith. The church begins to see that the faith journey is important to keep persons renewed. They see how important it is for new persons becoming part of the church and for long-time members staying active. Persons also discover or rediscover how vital such a faith journey is for themselves. Rather than narrowing the focus of the church, such exploration actually expands the focus and allows the gospel, in all its possibilities and implications, to guide the totality of life. A church in renewal begins to feel a fundamental sense of guidance by the inner life of the Spirit.

Energy arises out of faith formation and helps a congregation feel renewed from within. A united people of faith create energy for renewal. Renewal is a faith journey; renewal is itself ministry, as persons intentionally encourage one another in faith. Relying on the unconditional love of Christ is key to a congregation's growth. Every aspect of church renewal needs to be incorporated as an aspect of the faith journey. In fact, every movement of renewal in church history has been as individuals discovered the grace of God. From Paul's missionary journey to Luther's discovery of the grace of Christ to Bonhoeffer's call to participate in "costly grace," those who discover the deep meanings of God's presence are propelled to grow and discover the freedom and new life of the gospel. As personal faith grows, the church's atmosphere will change from despair to hope. A new heart and a new spirit for renewal are envisioned and experienced. It is to this specific plan for renewal that we now turn.

Chapter 3

Planning for Church Renewal

In order to move from the theoretical to the practical, we must establish a plan. In this chapter, we will develop a step-by-step process for establishing and implementing a plan of renewal. We will also look at specific issues that arise along the way. No plan of renewal is foolproof; continual correctives must be made as we experience God working. In fact, we should anticipate serendipitous moments in which renewal is experienced far beyond what we ever imagined. Maintaining a sense of expectancy and gratitude toward God keeps us humble and in an attitude of servanthood.

Our plan of renewal will develop as we match strengths with needs. Our aim is always transformation and growth. This part of the process requires careful thought. Like a sculptor who takes a rough stone and determines how to bring out its inherent beauty, we take the rough form of the present life of the church and formulate plans to shape it according to the beauty God calls forth from the members of the congregation. Each step calls for tapping the resources of the deepening faith and inner vitality of the congregation.

Envisioning Renewal

Background and Rationale

For the renewal process to begin, one of the first and most important tasks of leadership is envisioning renewal. Envisioning renewal means stepping back from the current situation of the church and seeing the calling of God to wholeness—how this congregation can be transformed by God to newness of life.

Leadership through this process requires both deep prayer and the ability to catch a vision for what can actually happen. The servant leader senses the promise present for new life and anticipates what is possible. The servant leader "hears things, sees things, knows things, and his [or her] intuitive insight is exceptional."[1] When putting together a puzzle, one develops a strategy, such as putting together the border first, then working on the clearly distinguishable areas, and finally tackling those difficult areas. Likewise, a leader in church renewal takes all the factors into account, looks at the big picture, and then identifies how to fit the pieces together—while always remembering that renewal often breaks forth spontaneously and beyond expectation. Rather than just reacting to the current pressing problems, the servant leader steps back in prayer and looks for God's promise of new life. Envisioning renewal is a strenuous but exhilarating art.

Step Toward Renewal #5

Have the renewal committee spend a focused time in prayer, seeking a vision for the congregation that is built on its strengths and is faithful to God's calling.

The question before the church at this point is, "Where is God calling our church just now?" The renewal committee, in one of its regular meetings, should have a time of intense prayer to seek the leading of the Holy Spirit on this question. Prayer is a vital aspect of renewal. In fact, my students, seeing how important this area of prayer is, wisely recommended that the focus on prayer, usually held toward the close of the church renewal course, be moved up toward the beginning. Jesus himself drew away for prayer and fasting at the beginning of his ministry, as well as when anticipating hardship (such as Luke 22:39-46) and seeking strength for his disciples (John 14:12-31). By helping his disciples see how God was with them, Jesus helped them catch a vision for the kingdom. In a similar way, nurturing our relationship with God helps us listen and become open to how God is reaching out to us. Envisioning renewal involves responding to God's love, which is searching us out and calling out a vision from us.

(In fact, a discipline of prayer is foundational to leadership and church renewal, for prayer is listening to God's movement. Renewal committee members, as well as all church members, should be encouraged, as part of the renewal process, to set aside time and establish a spiritual discipline of prayer. Many resources are available to guide us into a life of deeper prayer, from the daily lectionary Bible readings in the *Book of Common Prayer* to guided journals and books on prayer, a few of which are included in the bibliography. Listening to God is crucial not only in envisioning renewal but throughout its planning and implementation. Prayer helps us find direction when the way is not clear; prayer sets us in tune with renewal, with hope, with the gospel, and with inner joy.)

After its time of extended prayer, committee members should be encouraged to share freely any thoughts or hunches that come to them, no matter how small or large. These ideas should be recorded and reviewed for similarities and themes. By so doing, the next logical steps may begin to become clear; these initial ideas may actually be—but don't have to be—forerunners to the anticipated plan of renewal.

Bush Creek Church of the Brethren, the church with which I first worked on renewal, sensed it had strengths in teaching. Seeing a growing community around us and feeling our own need for renewal, we wondered where God was calling us. How could we reach out to new people? Did we have anything helpful or interesting to offer them? Much prayer and thought went into thinking about the future, and a vision began tugging at us. We decided that offering a solid Christian education plan would be important for both our growth and our service to the community. We had a sense that adults would not only want to have opportunities for their children to learn but would themselves want to grow. As new persons became actively involved in the church, they would need the background to teach and share their faith. This foresight meant that a new type of adult education—and teacher training—would be needed. Thus adult education became a natural focal point for congregational renewal.

As the vision unfolded, plans were made and then implemented for the adult elective class. A curriculum of courses was designed, with a Bible study one quarter, a study on a particular issue the next quarter, and a study of practical concern, like family life, the third quarter. A professional teacher trainer was enlisted, who asked to have twenty people for the class. In response, those most committed began to invite others to attend the teacher-training sessions, held first for teachers in all areas in general and then for teachers of adults in particular. The vision began to draw us. Using this excellent training, teams of teachers in the adult class began to teach a quarter at a time. They prepared well for their classes, using good resources and striving to balance teaching and discussion. They also emphasized the need for class members to support and encourage one another in their spiritual growth. Before long, children's Sunday school teachers wanted a break from teaching so that they could also participate in the adult classes! Soon the children and youth departments were also strengthened, not only by the teacher education offered but also by the enthusiasm of the adults.

We learned the vital balance of helping adults grow in their Christian life while nurturing the bond of fellowship in a growing community. Results far exceeded our expectations, and ultimately the Sunday school program became part of a successful multidenominational Sunday school study in the Mid-Atlantic region; we were later surprised but happy to learn that adult education was found to be one of the key common denominators in successful Sunday schools. Our vision was affirmed.

Another congregation had many widows in its midst, and home

visitation revealed that they were often alone and missing their loved ones. I sensed a need to help them deal with their loss and thereby feel more whole and productive. Several of the bereaved who responded that a group might be helpful to them were asked if they would contact other widows and widowers and invite them to a "grief group." One simple announcement appeared in the bulletin, and one announcement was made from the pulpit.

This effort was launched at the right time, in the right place, and for the right need. Again, the results went far beyond expectations. Fifteen showed up for the first meeting, at which we discussed the stages persons often experience in loss and considered spiritual themes and resources available to handle such feelings. The spiritual uplift was tremendous! For the next meeting, several people invited friends, and the group grew to twenty. Before long, those who had stayed at home began venturing out more, and individuals began to reach out to one another. For instance, when one member happened to see another member crying in the cemetery, she abandoned her plans to go shopping and instead stopped and offered friendship and support. By sensing needs, envisioning renewal, and establishing a program, this group experienced renewed spiritual life, neighborly outreach, and training for ministry. Along with all these benefits, this special program became known throughout the congregation and community, and the outpouring of love multiplied.

Envisioning renewal, therefore, is a process that evolves as individuals begin to sense God at work. Rather that just becoming busier, church members begin to sense that a vision is drawing their energies forward.[2] Catching a vision is crucial to thinking about church renewal. Rather than just responding to crises or to the immediate situation, the renewal committee can help facilitate long-term planning in the church by actively praying, reflecting on God's biblical calling for the congregation. It trusts that the God-given vision will become more and more clear as the first steps are taken in faith. Envisioning renewal is an intuitive process that draws on our prayer life, spiritual focus, and loving care of those we serve.

Outcomes

The primary outcome of envisioning renewal is that the church's ministry will be on target. By envisioning renewal and then responding with appropriate ministries, the church can begin to discover its mission. This will provide meaningful ministries rather than ones that will falter and create a deeper sense of failure. Members will begin to invest more time and energy because what is happening is meeting a need. People are fulfilled both in offering and receiving a ministry; they experience inner healing as ministries begin to accomplish the first steps of renewal.

As individuals feel growth in themselves and in others, they will invite friends and neighbors to come join them. They do not need to be prodded; they don't feel like they are being asked to prop up a failing program. In fact, many begin to take risks, volunteering to help in various ways and offering leadership that they used to feel unworthy to offer. As a result, everyone gains.

By envisioning renewal, servant leaders can see how results emerge naturally out of the strengths and potential of the congregation. Servant leaders do not overburden people by trying to tackle everything at once. Rather than forcing the development of ministries, a servant leader is sensitive to the ebb and flow of needs and schedules and the natural rhythms of life—for in reality the steps toward renewal do usually not happen in as clearly a sequential manner as outlined here. Renewal is an ongoing, fluid process directed by the Holy Spirit.

Matching Needs and Strengths

Background and Rationale

Much of what we have been talking about in setting up a plan of renewal brings us back to the triangle of renewal in Chapter Two, which diagrams the dynamic between biblical calling, God-given strengths, and evident need. We must now ask: "What exactly are the real needs of persons? Where do they hurt? What do they long for? What are they feeling most deeply in their lives right now?" Out of such questions, we can begin to match these needs with the strengths we've already identified.

By so doing, we find the very focus for renewal. For any endeavor to be successful, there must be a felt need. Otherwise, the program or project is only fulfilling self-interests, and it is going to take much effort to keep it going. Jesus always met felt needs. We can see how perceptive he was of the needs of those about him, whether it was of a tax collector up a tree or a woman touching the hem of his garment. The church needs to have its sensors out to perceive the needs of those who will welcome the Good News of the gospel. Perceiving which needs can be best met takes awareness and sensitivity.

Sometimes strengths or talents do not become evident until persons attempt to meet a need, until individuals rise to meet a need, only to discover the thrill of doing something they never imagined they could do. Persons often have a special avocation they'd like to put to use. Those who have obvious strengths may actually tire of always being asked to use them in the same way and would welcome a new challenge, while others may like to expand their expression of faith by using hidden or underdeveloped skills. Utilizing strengths to meet apparent needs can be an exciting endeavor.

Step Toward Renewal #6

Have the renewal committee attempt, in light of its prayer and discernment, to match the congregation's needs with its strengths.

While struggling to determine direction for the church, the question always arises, "How are we going to be able to do what we feel God wants done?" Rather than creating more work and more obligations, the best plan of renewal finds a way to match needs with strengths so that the needs are met by the identified strengths. Then people grow and faith grows—and the labor is a labor of love that energizes and fulfills. Therefore, thoughtful attention needs to be given to how the needs of the congregation can be met with its strengths.

One way to begin is to make a list of all the perceived needs. After servant leaders have listened and reflected carefully on the needs they see, a meeting could well be spent listing all of these. If a lengthy list is gathered, categorize the needs. The idea is not necessarily to identify as many needs as possible but to find the avenue by which the more pressing needs can be met. Not all the needs can be met, however. Some will seem more immediate; others more long range. Post this list next to the list of strengths so that committee members can discuss which combinations of needs and strengths would be logical and productive. Use your creativity to analyze these matches in terms of the steps to renewal that the committee has been exploring.

For example, in a congregation containing many children and younger youth, the parents were at various stages of involvement and spiritual life. The talents in this congregation were many, but it quickly became evident that some very skilled people did not have a way to fit in. So renewal began with identifying the need for a children's after-school club. The need and potential for such a group was great, but whoever would teach such a lively, energetic group? For one class of fifth and sixth graders, we knew of one very talented person who really didn't have a concrete way to use her talents. Although her work schedule was a concern, she had a good sense of humor, a keen mind, and a deep faith. What if this person was asked to teach in a team-teaching arrangement with the pastor? With a sense of the Spirit's leading, the renewal committee agreed to approach her. "Do you think I can really do it?" she asked. After discussion of the congregation's need and assurance of help in teaching and organizing, she responded favorably to the challenge.

The results were far better than anyone could have imagined! About twenty fifth and sixth graders were involved—a lively lot, especially when coming directly from school for the afternoon program! The four-fold youth program offers the model of recreation, a class, a service project, and a meal.[3] Each child has a sponsor, who serves as an integral part of the program and performs one of the many needed tasks, from transporting the young people to teaching to cooking the meal. Everyone has a part to play. The youth in return serve the church by singing in the Sunday morning worship service.

One day the new teacher brought to class a large wire-mesh figure in a kneeling position and materials for papier-mâché. As the young people gathered, she had them listen to a tape about the life of the apostle Paul while they draped wet strips of paper over the model. Besides working off excess energy, the event was both educational and fun. Afterwards, students remembered many details of this changed man. After they painted the papier-mâché figure, it was used as a worship center in the sanctuary in a service led by the youth club entitled "Paul: Such a Different Man." Everyone experienced the lesson of the miraculous transformation of one man by the gospel, and the shared impact of the youth club was tremendous.

Outcomes

One outcome of matching needs with strengths is that persons find fulfillment as proper matches are made. People grow because they are encouraged to meet those needs with their talents. Rather than just returning to last year's list of those who filled positions, the church calls on new persons and discovers new talents and opportunities. Creativity is expressed as new talents emerge. This entire process creates an excitement not present before. What a nice surprise to see someone in a new role and enjoying it!

At the same time, needs are also addressed. Keeping in mind the potential within the church, servant leaders see needs that, when met, can produce growth. As needs turn into opportunities, the church begins to discover the natural components to a plan of renewal, with ministries that evolve, one out of the other. Often the response to new ministries is to wonder why something was not done sooner. When needs are being met, the church will feel a responsiveness in ministry, and a movement of renewal has begun.

As individuals are called to respond, they begin to participate by matching their talent with an opportunity. A basic change of heart and feeling of satisfaction grow as those who minister find their calling and experience positive results. Both parties, those receiving the ministry and those called to provide leadership, benefit in the process. Church renewal and transformation happen at this important juncture. Like splicing together two lines so the current can flow, a plan of renewal that effectively matches needs and talents results in growth for everyone.

Setting Goals

Background and Rationale

After envisioning renewal and matching strengths with needs, a set of goals and an overall plan of renewal should be developed. This is to ensure that the renewal process has the benefit of systematic thought and planning over an extended period of time. Leaders are now in the position to help the church identify goals for the next several years.

The traditional method of goal setting is for church leaders and congregational representatives to go on a weekend retreat and develop a set of goals for the congregation. Although intentions are good, inherent in such a process are several weaknesses. The group often develops what amounts to a wish list—hopes of fixing whatever is not working without any workable plan to do so. This diagnostic model raises expectations that often are followed by disappointment, frustration, and blaming someone or something. In addition, high expectations are set without recognizing people's current needs and limitations. Building false hopes can result in even greater discouragement for a church.

In order to set realistic, workable goals, it is better to think in terms of where people are currently and where it is hoped they will be in a measurable time period. We define "goals" as the broad vision for the church, while "objectives" are the specific, measurable results that will help the church get there.[4] Goals can best be formulated by beginning with felt needs and appraised strengths. We should ask, "Where is God calling our congregation right now? How can persons more fully discover and live the gospel so that they are fulfilled and actively sharing the Good News?"

Step Toward Renewal #7

Have a congregational goal-planning session in order to set realistic goals, determine concrete objectives by which to accomplish them, and establish a reasonable timetable.

In order to establish a workable plan of renewal, the renewal committee brings its ideas for matching needs with strengths to a half-day congregational retreat or planning session. All those who are active in the work of the church should be encouraged to be present. The session should have an opening inspirational time followed by small groups in which members are asked: "Based on our identified strengths from the last meeting, what factors do you see that are leading us toward renewal as a church?" As these lists are brought together, the group should identify common threads of what is working and what is meaningful for the congregation. Next, have the group respond to the question: "How can these strengths be built on to meet felt needs?" The aim is to help the group find workable ways to build on what is exciting and meaningful to them. At some point the renewal committee should share its ideas on matching needs and strengths, some of which should be similar to what the total group has been finding. These potential steps toward renewal need to be affirmed.

As one or two directions become clear, establish a specific goal and a set of objectives for action. Keep in mind that most changes take at least three years, and set the goals and objectives within a realistic time frame. Use newsprint to place your workable, attainable, and practical objectives on a time line so that the plan of renewal is clear to all. A goal statement could be developed and placed at the end of each stage of development listed.

Do not set a goal to fill the pews; set other goals, and growth is likely to follow. While at first Bush Creek had no formal plan for renewal, our church's initial emphasis was to let people moving into the neighborhood know that our church was active and a place where they could grow spiritually. We knew that our old, closed-up, front-entry door made our church building look unused. While a skilled woodworker in the congregation made three attractive new signs for the church, I began making several visits a week to new neighbors in order to discover what needs I could meet on the visit itself as well as let them know what the church was doing. We soon began a quarterly community newsletter in order to inform neighbors about ministries like vacation Bible school, and the board opened the church building to a new community organization working on citizens' concerns. As pastor I learned that a weekly article concerning worship and special events was welcomed by the county newspaper. In about a year, no longer did our church members hear remarks about our church being closed. In fact, new neighbors began attending and meeting others who soon became friends.

Outcomes

Clear goals and concrete objectives will emerge from matching needs and strengths. Careful, specific planning can help renewal happen in small, measurable steps. As people begin to see what can happen and respond to the vision in tangible ways, the church will move forward and grow.

Establishing goals for a plan of renewal also unites a congregation. People come to church with a variety of different interests and concerns, and the implementation of goals can make use of a wide variety of strengths and talents among the people. Having goals sets the tone for something important to come, and people feel they are a part of the church's future as they feel ownership at the ground floor of the plan.

Another outcome is that, before a retreat or congregational goal-setting meeting is over, a concrete plan of renewal begins to emerge. The plan may not be totally set because further research may be needed on what resources are available and what kinds of similar programs have been tried elsewhere. Further work may also need to be done in very specific areas in order to find how goals can be implemented, and neighboring churches or a regional office may need to be consulted. But rather than unrealistic wish lists, working goals have been set that can lead to greater ease in establishing a plan of renewal.

Establishing a Plan of Renewal
Background and Rationale

Often a plan of renewal is a prepackaged commodity that is to bring calculated results: if we will just follow the plan, we are told, the results are guaranteed. Not so for our plan of renewal! As anyone who implements this process will learn, much effort and forethought is entailed in establishing a plan of renewal that considers all the human qualities and experiences of a congregation. Sometimes it is through hardship and failure that we learn what the Christian faith really entails in terms of trust, understanding, and forgiveness. A plan of renewal is an attempt to be faithful to the gospel in our own context, with our congregation's particular needs and strengths.

A plan of renewal is therefore a response and not a grand design. Persons build on what they feel will work. They are willing to make the investment needed if they can envision a beneficial outcome. If a plan is solid, they will feel it is worthy of their time and effort and even develop a certain sense of pride in it. Ownership by a wide range of people is of central importance. Most successful endeavors have clear expectations; a plan for renewal serves as a kind of road map to help us get to our intended destination.

Such a plan draws together all that has been said and plots out a step-by-step process for renewal. It should have a central thrust, with small steps that build on one another. Establishing a plan of renewal involves focusing a church's efforts on wherever new life is emerging. It is important to see how such a plan can unfold both intentionally and naturally.

Step Toward Renewal #8

The committee establishes a plan of renewal to be in some way formalized with the entire congregation and dedicated at a Sunday morning worship service.

The renewal committee should now sketch out a three-year plan that draws together all that has been said. It should have a central thrust, with small steps of implementation that build logically on one another. Establishing a plan of renewal means focusing the church's efforts at a point where new life can emerge from strengths meeting needs. Ask, "What is the logical first step? While everything may seem urgent, what priorities can we set? How can one step become the building block for the next step?" Next, establish an official long-term time line, writing in goals, objectives, and specific steps to be taken. The three-year period may best be broken down into six three- to six-month blocks of spring and fall sessions, although summer and winter may certainly also be significant times of renewal and other time periods may better suit your congregation's calendar year. Although eager for renewal by now, the committee and the congregation will need to recognize the need for patience. Needed changes, new ways of operating, and adjustments to the new life will take time—but they will be worth waiting for!

In Bush Creek Church of the Brethren's plan of ministry, a group of persons guided me as pastor in responding to the goals, and a supervisory group of pastors took time out of their monthly meeting to give input and guidance. Stated goals were translated into an overall vision put at the end of a time line; intended end results were listed, and various steps for accomplishing them were specified so that events could be planned months ahead of time. As a focus of ministry was formulated for each area of renewal, three concrete areas developed: spiritual renewal, organizational renewal, and a faith/love emphasis both within the congregation and to those outside the church. Some areas were rather nebulous at first; others were altered as plans proceeded. The result, however, was a plan of renewal that attained its goals.

In the area of spiritual renewal, the church decided to continue its successful experience with "lay witnesses" coming from other churches and sharing their faith. As faith became more real and more practical through this sharing, people claimed greater ownership of their own spiritual growth. In this case, after two lay-witness weekends, the church decided to design its own annual spiritual retreat experience in the local church setting. Such ownership for spiritual growth went way beyond what was planned and truly implemented the original goal of each taking ownership and discovering faith in Christ as a reality.

Organizational renewal was also seen as key to the plan of ministry. New people needed to feel that they were a part of the church and sense that the church was working together on various ministries. Having shorter, more focused board meetings with clear agendas made the organization more intentional and helped the board and various committees develop a sense of confidence and accomplishment. More time and energy was invested in planning and implementing the work of the committees on a weekly basis, and the church as an organization began functioning effectively and drew in more and more people.

Finally, in the faith/love emphasis, a potpourri of areas indicated a desire for an increase in genuine love and reaching out to others. The genius of the plan of renewal was that each effort would unfold in its own time, and each program effort would dovetail into the next. A forty-days-of-love emphasis was done to help persons reach out to others. A pictorial directory helped the congregation get to know both new and old members. Individuals' gifts were celebrated and put to use at services. The outreach ministry of the church grew significantly, with various hunger projects, collections for disasters, and a clothing room for persons in need in the community. Such a serving congregation began to draw persons together.

This plan of ministry had both strengths and weaknesses. One strength was the specific response made to areas of need in the church. Persons felt that their faith was more real, programs had more ownership, and the old identity of "unfriendly church" faded. Furthermore, the plan gave members a sense of purpose. It is no accident that a youth ministry emerged during this process. At the time of the plan, some wondered how such a youth ministry would ever be possible, but it happened. Finally, the plan guided me as pastor not only in my own pastoral ministry but also in formulating marks of ministry that would determine the spirit and direction of the congregation.[5]

The plan's weaknesses included a chart so global that it lost its thrust by trying to respond to too many needs at once. In retrospect, one focus would have been better than three, although in this case they happened at different times of the year. Also, the objectives could have been more realistic. In retrospect, the plan leaned toward a heavy agenda and needed tempering. This indeed happened, however, and everyone felt more comfortable. Finally, the plan was weak in terms of understanding the nature of change. Since growth takes time and often comes in unexpected ways, a redirection in course had to be made from time to time.

Overall, however, the church knew it was on the way, as outcomes far exceeded expectations in many cases. Flexibility was a necessary by-product of growth, and problems were faced from a position of strength so that everyone felt good about the results. Renewal was experienced as the exciting results of their planning and labors were shared as a church community.

How to best formalize the plan of renewal will vary from congregation to congregation. Beware that setting too formal a course may impede the renewal process and relegate it as another church program to be handled solely by a committee; the plan of renewal *will* change as it emerges. (Too much formalization at this point can actually move the thrust away from the vision for renewal, which should incorporate all that happens in the life of the church. In Chapter 8, we will look at how such subtle shifts can begin downward spirals.) For renewal to occur, focus must be retained on God's working within people's lives. The plan of renewal should be seen as leaven that will permeate the whole life of the church.

To dedicate and formalize the plan of renewal, therefore, may be to find some way to celebrate the new life emerging. The vision of new life can be celebrated with some service of consecration. Symbols can often be a part of such a process. At Bush Creek Church of the Brethren, a special symbolic cornerstone made of cinder block was used as a "worship center" for renewal. A wood crafter fashioned a Chi Rho (the first two Greek letters for the word *Christ)* out of fine plywood, which was set up inside the block. We then celebrated Christ as the cornerstone upon which the church was built, as our new life in Christ was calling us and shaping us as a people. The pastor of the Mayfair Conwell Memorial Church used a potted tree from her office as a symbol of renewal. As part of a Sunday worship service, something visual and symbolic may be dedicated as a life-giving, expanding image of renewal.

You may or may not choose to have a more formal presentation of the plan of renewal. In Bush Creek's plan of ministry, the seminary, the church, and I as pastor entered into a formal agreement to express a commitment to making renewal a priority. In this case, this was a very important step of mutual commitment. Formalization or dedication can involve enlisting the prayers and mutual support of the congregation during part of the regular worship service, or can be done as a special service, with a sermon on renewal and a dedication of leaders and emerging ministries. The key is to focus on new life emerging rather than on a program. The congregation can then draw together in support of the vision that has been based on its self-identified strengths.

Outcomes

An overall plan unfolds naturally as the way for growth becomes clear. A step-by-step plan is not an agenda set in stone but is a means of creating momentum. As people get excited, renewal becomes contagious. Once the trend toward renewal begins, a growing momentum is felt by all.

Another outcome is that, as new strengths emerge, the group is actually able to achieve goals that weren't even considered possible before. A working plan of renewal emerges from the lives of people, and such a plan is usually realistic. The simple but thorough nature of the planning process makes implementation much easier.

A third significant outcome is that aspects of new life can be lifted up as an ongoing process of renewal. Rather than just one service of dedication, the pastor or renewal committee can highlight new life emerging in the church as a means of continual encouragement. The worship service becomes a place to dedicate new and old ministries alike, encourage one another in spiritual growth and service, and give thanks for signs and symbols of new life. People feel ownership as new life comes into being, and, as the unbinding of potential occurs, a new heart and a new spirit emerge.

In the next chapter, we will look at how to actually implement our established plan of renewal.

Chapter 4

Implementing the Plan of Renewal

After matching needs with strengths, setting goals, and establishing a plan, the next step is rather obvious: implementing the plan of renewal. No matter how obvious, however, many efforts fall short at this stage, for indeed, here the hard work begins. Implementing a plan takes time, energy, and patience. If plans start to get bogged down or off track, some may be tempted to give up, saying, "Well, it looked good on paper."

The good news is that nothing in the plan of renewal is set in concrete. The renewal committee can facilitate implementation of the plan of renewal by periodically evaluating and modifying the plan as necessary; it can help those in leadership articulate their needs and concerns and see alternatives when the original plan isn't working. A three-year renewal plan calls for patience, strength, forbearance, and creativity as new attempts and redirections are made.

Having already established and dedicated its plan of renewal, the congregation, well aware of its commitment to growth, will probably feel that further work needs to be done to bring the plan to fruition. Often training will be needed for those involved in new ministries, as well as encouragement and guidance along the way. Other topics related to renewal will need to be addressed as the congregation grows. Short-term emphases usually yield only short-term gains; long-term renewal happens with long-term, focused efforts. Implementing a plan of renewal over a three-year period therefore helps growth to be more than temporary.

Setting Up a Ministry

Background and Rationale

Much effort goes into setting up a ministry. First, to organize any new initiative, available persons and resources must be identified. It must also be determined how this ministry will fit not only into the life of the church but also into the lives of those with whom this ministry is done. A new ministry needs to be done at the right time, in the right place, and in the right spirit. For instance, if the ministry involves adults, what will any children be doing during this time? If this ministry is for children, what will adults be doing who transport them? The best plans use the maximum number of strengths and have a minimum number of conflicts; they are "user-friendly." While commitment is necessary, convenience, manageability, and suitability are also important to a plan's success.

Setting up a manageable ministry therefore requires great sensitivity to the needs of others. Persons in ministry must negotiate ways to create the least number of disruptions and conflicts. We can view this organizing work as ministry itself, for persons are making new commitments and giving up old routines in order to grow in their faith and serve others. Interpreting the journey through spoken and written word are very important, for new precedents are being established and new memories created; a new heart and a new spirit are in formation.

Step Toward Renewal #9

Gather together the people who can make this ministry work by setting a course of action.

Who are the key people who can make this effort work? They are those with vested interests, those who will benefit, those who may not usually be considered but have some untapped talent that can be drawn on. With them the renewal committee should share the details of the vision thus far. This is a time to build support, to lay the essential groundwork for action. Information and ideas can be shared by drawing on the experiences of others. Some programs, such as Youth Club International, come with a cassette tape that describes the program and details what is needed.[1] Perhaps resource persons from area churches with a ministry similar to the one you have envisioned could help your church get started. In any case, the ministry needs to help its members grow in depth spiritually and in breadth in love and service. Make sure that those involved clearly understand what will be required to accomplish the ministry. If it seems unfeasible, do not proceed. Why add another defeat to the church?

After beginning consultation with one large church, I could tell that something special was happening that gave the people an unusual closeness. It came through on the questionnaires and in the phone contacts. I soon learned that the church had a very active "shepherding program." The congregation had been divided into small groups that met periodically with leaders called "shepherds," who received special training during the Sunday school hour and helped persons care for one another. Members' concerns were shared and prayed for via an active telephone network. A vision was clearly in operation; the church had organized a ministry that offered enormous benefits for the congregation. Out of a dream to have persons be supportive of one another, a workable ministry was providing renewal on a regular basis.

What might be needed to set up such a ministry? First, it seems, a need would be felt. Next, there would be a vision and a person who wanted to see it through. Because accomplishing the goal would involve everyone in the congregation, the vision would need to be taken to the people in order to enlist the broadest support possible. A feasibility study could be done to ensure that this large an undertaking could actually be translated into a workable model of ministry. Next, a planning group could gather together to design an overall plan, including how to train leaders and organize the actual groups. A time line could be drawn up to determine when to begin, when to organize the groups, when to train the leaders, and when to obtain any resources for the groups. Finally, the practical work of implementation would begin. Persons implementing the program could determine how best to divide the congregation into shepherding groups, knowing that adjustments would be needed for the most effective, ongoing support. A key to successful implementation would be interpreting what benefit such a ministry would have in terms of Christian growth, mutual support, and outreach to others. Even as the groups were established, continued work would need to be done to maintain such a ministry. The committee would have to check periodically with group leaders and random members to see that all was going well. The shepherding class, itself a ministry, might offer a good and regular way to support group leaders.

Outcomes

As a ministry is founded, a new force is established within a congregation. New relationships are formed as the power of the gospel speaks to people's needs. If the ministry is given a name, a new entity has also been established. Some may feel left out, so avenues must be created for them either to become involved or to find their own niche. Others will be quietly supportive, giving the encouragement that any program needs. If the new ministry has no formal organization and is done more individually, regular updates and reports will help others know how to be supportive.

Like having a new baby in the house, a new ministry brings changes. In preparing for it, there is joy and excitement. The focus of a lot of attention, this new ministry will take time to emerge, however, and persons need time to integrate the new being into the family. Some may feel the new ministry will take away from them, that there will be less time or resources for them. On the other hand, they may see the benefits and discover that the new life is exciting. As new growth occurs, the family picture will change. The old will be remembered, while new memories will also be made. This can be an exciting time of making new history. A new ministry can enrich other ministries in the church as strength encourages strength, and ultimately other areas of the church will experience growth as well.

Another outcome of establishing a new ministry is that movement is felt, movement that is positive and focused. When something constructive is occurring, people feel that they have a way to grow in faith. Discussions of malaise in the church can be replaced by discussions of the life happening in the new ministry. That is very healthy; new life is emerging. Persons even begin to enjoy attending meetings and stop looking at their watches every few minutes! The church gains a confidence for its life and direction and begins to feel more confident about the future. In a real way, the posture of such a church changes because renewal is moving it from general discussion to focused action.

Enlisting

Background and Rationale

Crucial to setting up a new ministry is enlisting individuals. The priority we give to our manner of enlisting will directly correlate to the importance persons attach to being asked to participate in a ministry. For instance, as a pastor I would never try to enlist someone for a position on a Sunday morning because most people come to church on Sunday to study and worship, not to be asked to do something. Secondly, I would never ask someone to do something during a home visit unless that was clearly the mutually understood purpose of the visit or a new ministry happened to address a person's expressed need.

I found that the best approach to enlisting was to set up a visit in which we both intended to discuss possible involvement in a certain ministry. To enlist someone for a ministry requires a carefully thought-out approach that includes identifying talents and having the needed material resources to accomplish the ministry. At the onset of his ministry, Jesus called some fishermen by name to follow him and thus redefined their focus for life. Whether they had met Jesus before or not we do not know, but they were clearly ready to respond. Thoughtful prayer of servant leaders can help identify the points of readiness in members of the congregation. Then individuals can be approached with a possible call for their lives to be used in service. Such a call to discipleship moves us from commitment in general to commitment in particular. Here is presented an opportunity for new growth that can bring much fulfillment. Some room for a negative response should be given, but proper timing and patience can often yield a yes, particularly if training and guidance (to be considered in greater detail in the next section) is offered.

Step Toward Renewal #10

Meet with persons invited to be part of the new ministry and build enthusiasm, share a calling, and enlist their help in clear and specific ways.

In a relaxed atmosphere, sit down together to consider a mutual sense of calling to a particular ministry. The discussion must be conducted with understanding and sensitivity, and room for objections, questions, fears, or concerns should be given. When in seminary, I will never forget when, near the end of my ministerial training, I went to one of my major advisors and expressed that I was not sure that the ministry was for me. Did I really have what it would take? He responded immediately, saying, "That's good! You stand in the great prophetic call tradition. Look at the prophets. They all felt they did not have what it would take." We need to keep in mind that when we ask persons to serve, they may have hesitations. We need to express that we feel they have something special to offer: "We come because we have seen a potential within you." This visit is not to fill a vacant spot. It is to challenge a person to grow because of identified potential.

Enlisting individuals requires finding places—"people spots"—where they will not only fit in and function but will grow. This is true whether calling people to leadership or to participate in the church in general. James Moss, who developed the concept of "people spots," suggests that a "people spot" includes three things: a physical place like a chair or spot in the pew, a place where relationships can develop, and a place where felt needs are met. "People spots" are often full, and assertive efforts must be made to create new ones. In starting a new ministry, many persons must often be approached just to have a workable group. To grow, churches must make a concerted effort not only to attract but also assimilate new members into their own "people spots"—a place to belong.[2]

Outcomes

Each effort in enlisting is an opportunity to call a person into a deeper relationship with Christ. Each effort can be seen as an opportunity to meet people's particular needs and tap their unique talents as well as to interpret an important new ministry. Each effort can be seen as an opportunity to create the overall spirit of renewal. No effort in enlisting is wasted; sometimes the seed is simply planted, and persons need time in order to allow the new life to emerge. If immediate results are not seen, long-term results may be realized years later. The work of enlisting is strenuous. A lot of patience and love are required, but no work is more essential and more rewarding.

A valuable outcome of enlisting is putting people's gifts to use. Seeing the potential within individuals, we help them feel affirmed and valued. Persons come to believe, maybe for the first time, they have gifts that are useful.[3] To help persons develop their gifts and grow in their ministries, the Alban Institute suggests employing a coordinator of lay volunteers. As a church explores how persons can use their gifts, such a position may well develop. Or the personnel committee may fulfill this function. It can, in fact, become one of the most active committees in the church, identifying needs for leadership, getting to know people, and enlisting them to serve in ministries. People begin to feel a part of a church that is calling them forth in Christ's service.

Another outcome is that the same persons are not asked over and over again to do a certain ministry. Rather than beginning with whoever did something last year, the process of enlisting begins with which persons can most meaningfully meet the identified need. If an individual really enjoys a ministry but another person is also suited, a natural teaming of the two can be very effective. Training, whether formal or informal, can effectively develop gifts and reinforce the process of growth. A supervision process can also be developed so that persons don't flounder while expressing their new talents (see Chapter 5). The outcome of enlisting can therefore be a vital part of the entire process of renewal.

Training

Background and Rationale

On the heels of enlisting comes training. Such training should be not only for the recognized leaders but also for assistants and others who would respond to an invitation for training. Training is actually an extension of enlisting because it gives persons the tools to do the task requested. As confidence is built, success is more likely. Training is therefore more than just an annual event; it requires setting up a process of growth that will help persons develop in their ministries. Training is part of what we give to persons to help them give to others. Training is essential for the church to be alive and energetic in its witness.

Step Toward Renewal #11

The renewal committee establishes ongoing training to help persons grow in their ministries.

Each type of ministry requires a different type of training. Basic to all ministries is an understanding of the biblical tradition, the beliefs of the church, and how the local congregation operates. Beyond that are the unique understandings and skills needed to bolster the confidence of those called to the particular ministry. The renewal committee will need to explore what resources are available and apt to be most helpful. Often persons must begin to implement their ministries before being able to determine what further training will be most helpful. Some training can be done via books or articles; some can be done via training events tailored to the local situation. In either case, the investment in training will be well worth the effort.

At Bush Creek we learned a lot about training through developing a teacher-training series. Robert McLaughlin, our hired professional trainer, emphasized that such training would be a time saver; his hope was to have teachers develop several lesson plans during the classes. He required that at least twenty persons be present for the class; therefore, interested persons actively enlisted other church members to participate in the class (several of whom became truly interested in the process and found a new confidence to teach). Each training session, like Jesus' parables, was focused on one main point, upon which a teacher could expand in his or her lesson. The training sessions were held at the church itself—making it easier for members to attend and envision their learnings applied to their familiar surroundings. Also, by limiting participation to our own members, a fellowship of support was developed and carried into the weeks and months ahead; persons began to share their growth with one another and help one another.

Training should not be thought of as just for teachers. In one congregation, the ushers got together for a monthly breakfast and had a training session. A tremendous esprit de corp grew among the team of ushers as they took pride in being good hosts and hostesses to persons coming to worship. Training could be offered to nursery workers, youth leaders, small group leaders, deacons, board members, new member sponsors, prayer group leaders, and so on. Training materials are available for many of these areas, although you may have to search for them or update and tailor them for your particular congregation. Asking other congregations to help locate talented persons to lead a training session can be fruitful, and the interchange itself can be affirming and life giving.

At Bush Creek, two other areas of training were addressed. One was to train persons to supervise the pastor. Because such supervision is unique, this meant informing persons how to give helpful feedback. Such supervision would monitor how to keep balance, how to keep the plan working, and how to make adjustments. Interestingly, persons came to like playing such a role. They felt they could provide a vital function for leadership if the pastor was willing to ask for help. The other area of training was for the youth counselors in the youth ministry, which grew beyond the original expectations. Youth advisors told us what they felt they needed to feel more confident in their work. We had to do a lot of work to find the best options to help them become confident leaders and assistants. Training materials were harder to find, but we learned that some of the older materials, while dated, were actually more practical for our situation.

Training objectives should be set in the same way we set the objectives for the plan of renewal. Just as we began with where the congregation was at the time and plotted a course to help fulfill their vision, so in training we begin with where persons presently are and, without judging them, aim to help them become all they can become. When designing sessions or finding materials, those in leadership need to think of equipping persons for their specific ministry. Training can be exciting, and the leadership developed in a congregation can far exceed what was ever dreamed possible. When talents and treasures are no longer hidden, persons can become confident, reliable, and effective leaders in a ministry of renewal.

Outcomes

The outcomes of training are many. Not only are persons given the skills they need, but an intentionality spreads to the entire ministry of the congregation. Individuals take on a new self-confidence that makes everyone feel better. Training helps in enlisting other persons because it builds enthusiasm. Often other persons attend the sessions, if only to provide refreshments or clean up the building. Involvement increases; persons learn and grow. Training helps persons release their creativity and feel good about growing in ministry.

Good training helps persons over time. As many high schools, colleges, and extension services offer training to adults, the church can provide vital leadership education that offers new meaning to life. With concrete ideas sparked by creativity, training helps persons develop their personal ministry. They begin to find that they can do things they never dreamed were possible. Through learning about available resources, their whole world of learning is opened up. Often those very resources are ones to which they turn later when situations arise that call for creative responses. Persons also find the value of supporting others who are trying new things—just as they tried new things. Training can open new avenues of spiritual and personal growth as well as development of skills and mutual support for ministry.

Starting the Ministry

Background and Rationale

Being ready to start a ministry feels tremendous! Whether it is a new youth club, a ministry for singles, or a new emphasis on worship, the inauguration of any effort is a high point. Even if we don't have as many persons involved as we had envisioned, we must remember that kingdom growth is at first thirty fold, then sixty fold—and the value of each person is immeasurable. All of our plans have aimed for the moment of the ministry's launching. A lot of ground work has been laid; the end product is the result of many intentional small steps. At this point, rather than oversell the product, leaders should focus instead on serving the immediate needs of others and letting the ministry speak for itself.

Step Toward Renewal #12

After the planning and training process is complete, start the ministry.

Any major thrust for renewal is the culmination of at least six months of planning. For example, if a ministry is being projected for the fall, planning should begin before Lent, in the winter months of that year. Lay out the preliminary plans before the Lenten season begins, so that as Lent and Easter plans require immediate attention at one level, behind-the-scenes planning for the new endeavor can be done on another level—need assessment, resource availability, input from key individuals. After Easter, major planning can then be taken up before summer, when persons go on vacation and are not interested in too many meetings. With organized long-range planning, the fall can be greeted with anticipation rather than with frantic scrambling to prepare for the new ministry's launch.

Adequate notice needs to be given regarding when the new ministry will begin. Three or four notices in a variety of forms are needed, since some persons are verbal and some are visual. Some communication needs to be done informally by word of mouth. Perhaps one person will invite another—or even better, bring someone along. Some persons like to be "charter members"; others may be hesitant at first and want to see how a ministry goes before joining in. Persons must be made to feel welcome in their own time. In all your communications, highlight the positive results of the new ministry, as these can be some of the best publicity—and encouragement to those already involved.

Beginning a ministry is a practical endeavor. All things need to be well organized for a program to operate: the necessary materials must be ordered; if there are refreshments, they need to be readied; the heat and lights need to be on; erasers should be handy if needed. It is best to walk through the plans from beginning to end to ensure that as many factors as possible have been handled beforehand, thus maximizing the potential for the ministry's success. The prayers of the congregation, as well as their active support, should also be enlisted to help the endeavor in every way possible. When starting up a new class, I would always carry extra curriculum pieces on my home visits and attempt to share what plans were being made to help persons grow in their faith. Adequate excitement must be generated in order to have such a project bear fruit.

Part of the plan of implementation needs to include celebration. This is more than just a party; it is recognition of efforts accomplished, of persons' contributions, of growth in faith. Rather than occupying another evening, such recognition can be with a certificate on a Sunday morning or with a personal letter of appreciation; thank-you notes are a real morale booster. Also, celebration can be a time for a needed pause. Rather than diving immediately into the next step of the plan of renewal, persons often need a break, an opportunity to rest and give some time to other loyalties, and to get ready for the next phase of work. Renewal over the long haul involves pacing oneself, just like in a long-distance race. Endurance builds as persons share the load with one another and allow one another to be refreshed for the next lap. Celebrate that persons are growing in faith as they plan and serve. Regular worship services can become a time for this celebration, bringing renewal to meet the challenges week by week. Renewal is then celebrated and affirmed.

Outcomes

With the implementation of ministry, transformation and growth is seen as persons' lives are changed. Individuals feel that real needs are being addressed and strengths utilized. They can begin to identify strengths within themselves they didn't realize they had. They sense that God is at work in their lives.

Persons also begin to affirm the corporate church because something meaningful is happening, something in which they feel invested. The church has a vision that is being implemented. The new ministry, which effectively matches needs with strengths, is apt to feel very natural. New landmarks are being laid and new traditions established. Better communication is taking place as needs are met and people are growing in faith and learning to depend on God's leading and strength to provide ministry. While growth can be scary and at times painful—as can unbinding for new life—there is a strong sense of joy in working together in a process that requires joint efforts. New life comes forth, and the resurrection is experienced. A new heart and a new spirit emerge!

Chapter 5

Supervising Persons in Renewal

Once a new ministry is begun, we cannot abandon the persons launching it, lest the total renewal process be short-circuited. The servant leader will recognize that individuals need ongoing supervision in order for long-term growth to occur. A method of supervision is called for that can effectively help persons grow in their ministry as well as in their faith. Supervision is the key to the ongoing renewal of the church, as persons learn to respond to needs by becoming more sensitive to, more equipped for, and more confident in the tasks at hand.[1]

Supervision

Background and Rationale

The manner of this supervision is of key importance. Supervision is not one person telling another what to do; rather, supervision is one person affirming the growth areas of another and helping that person come to a greater fullness of expression of their talents. The supervisor *does* accept a kind of authority, however, in guiding someone else who is growing in ministry. Supervision means specific approaches, sensitive responses, and a long-term investment. If a plan of ministry is to come to fruition, key leaders must be carefully supervised as they guide the new ministry.[2]

In this chapter we will explore how a contract can be formed that outlines how such help will be provided. The supervisor will meet with the new leader for approximately six sessions of forty-five minutes in length as a new ministry is launched. These could taper off, with a year-end check-in. With a contract we become specific in defining a helping relationship, how long it will last, what will be done, and what outcomes one hopes to achieve. Supervision helps persons identify obstacles and find creative approaches in ministry. Supervision also helps persons discover ever more clearly God's purpose and activity in their lives.

Spiritual formation frequently happens as persons enter into ministry. Teachers often say that they learn the most when they teach. In the same manner, whether that ministry be teaching, leading youth, or doing daily life ministry, we come to trust ever more deeply in God, to learn of God's grace, and to feel God's movement in our lives as we implement our ministry.

Step Toward Renewal #13

The renewal committee assigns a person to engage in a supervision process with the leader(s) of the new ministry.

The renewal committee can call on either the pastors or key lay leaders to engage in a supervision process, which is built around the training done for leaders in ministries. Such sessions are set to help keep persons from feeling that once they have been called and said yes, they are on their own. The supervision process calls forth their best talents and ensures that they will receive help. In the supervision process detailed here, the learnings in faith are lifted up so that to engage in ministry means to be growing in faith. Supervisors should initially set up monthly sessions of approximately forty-five minutes for a period of about four months. Such supervision is an investment, to be sure, but may also be thought of as some of the best training that can be done.

The renewal committee may decide to cut its meetings in half in order to provide the valuable work of supervision. Also, the renewal committee at some point may wish to do such supervision with a group of persons who gather to share their growth and their problems. The intent of supervision is support and encouragement so that persons can grow into their ministries. Such supervision can be seen as an integral part of implementing the plan of ministry. Here, burnout is short-circuited and growth is encouraged. When the initial enthusiasm begins to wear thin, the supervision process can offset premature fatigue. Such supervision is like planting a seed so that a new heart and a new spirit can take hold and grow.

Listening

The first step in supervision is listening. In the first session the supervisor can ask the person in ministry, "How are things going?" Usually this is enough to help persons initiate dialogue. If trust is present, they may relate what is happening within them as well as what is happening in the ministry. Listening plays a crucial role in that it allows persons to explore just what they are feeling without any threat. New leaders can share the excitement of what is happening as well as any disappointment or fear with what they feel is not happening. A listening supervisor offers an attentive ear and understanding. A supervisor may ask a question such as, "Do I hear you saying . . . ?" in order to find out what a person is feeling. Listening also shows that someone is concerned and helps leaders clarify for themselves what is happening. A sharing of the experience can then occur.

Several things happen in listening. Listening has a way of affirming another in ministry. It says that this ministry is important—someone wants to hear about it! Such a feeling can be conveyed in a multitude of ways in supervision. Simple comments and nods can help, as well as words that show understanding, appreciation, and identification. Each reflection can be affirming, conveying to the leaders that what they are experiencing is valid. The fact that someone else takes this ministry seriously means a lot. In listening, the supervisor identifies strengths that can be affirmed as well as areas of growth that a leader wants to explore. Confirmation through listening becomes a stepping stone for growth.

"So if I hear you right, Susan, you like your new-found work with the youth club, but it stretches your patience when the children get overly active, and sometimes you feel you don't have enough biblical knowledge when the children ask you questions." Such a comment could be a very sensitive and discerning response to a youth club teacher. Active listening enables persons to make new observations for themselves about their own experience. They are able to summarize, take a breather, affirm, and evaluate. Support and encouragement can often be rendered through listening. Listening lays the important groundwork for all that is to follow.

How is such listening most helpfully done? Supervisors listen with their whole being. The supervisor notes nuances of meanings, body language, and faith expressions that come through. The supervisor may paraphrase what he or she hears. In listening, it is also appropriate to make comments such as: "You really have been engaged in interesting work, haven't you?" "The singles group has had some low moments and some high moments." "I am impressed with the sincerity and the devotion with which you have been working."

Conversations should be held in confidence so that the individual feels free to share. Such confidentiality sets the stage for growth. A person is at this point today; tomorrow can be different. If times have been exasperating, a good process of supervision can help a person find a new approach to the situation.

Listening begins the process of attentiveness to what God is doing. Quietness, receptiveness, and searching are important aspects of these conversations. Persons are able to talk about things that others in ministry felt long before them. Like Elijah, they can draw away in quiet refuge and hear again the quiet prompting of God. Listening can help persons explore new areas, heretofore undiscovered, where God is at work. Listening begins to raise intentionality about what leaders are doing and helps them focus on what may otherwise become either routine or too stressful. Listening can help persons hear what God is saying. Sometimes it is not in the dramatic events like in the earthquake, wind, and fire that God is discovered but in the ways of hushed stillness.

Identifying Growth Areas

A second step in supervision is to create support around primary growth areas. The supervisor begins doing this by supporting the ministry of another in general. By listening and by encouraging, the supervisor helps a person identify where growth may occur. Perhaps one topic keeps reemerging. A question is posed; a dilemma is present. The supervisor works to help the person identify these areas. The supervisor may ask the person what is meant in a certain area. Identifying, clarifying, and summarizing are all important functions of the supervisor.

At that moment the one doing supervision should resist the temptation to offer advice. It is often too easy to tell persons what they could do differently. That time may come, as trust builds and suggestions can be made. However, people can quickly build walls of resistance or feel like giving up if "the expert" is too quick to point out their failures. Instant advice can short-circuit the supervision process. Also, such an arrangement can set up the dynamic of expert and novice whereby the new leader always runs to the supervisor for advice. Instead, if the supervisor identifies areas in which the individual wishes to grow, a sense of ownership is built for those being supervised and the initiative is kept in their hands.

In light of the above, a person may say, "I want to grow in my biblical knowledge first because then I will not feel as nervous. I also want to do a prayer discipline at least twice a week to grow in patience and in awareness of God's leading." This person can then use these supervision sessions to learn how to deal creatively in ministry.

The supervisor needs to do adequate homework by studying and conferring about the area of ministry for which he or she is offering supervision. Not being able to provide all the answers should not preclude becoming knowledgeable in the area. Supervision is a combination of information and interaction. A leader's growth should not be limited to personal issues due to a supervisor's lack of familiarity with the area of ministry. A sense of training should pervade as the supervisor attempts to help a leader grow in his or her area of ministry.

The overriding intent in identifying areas for growth is to reinforce the approach of coming from our strengths. From that vantage point, we can work gently on perceived weaknesses. The supervisor may affirm that achievement has come in one area and help identify growth that can follow in another. Without belaboring the point, the ability to build a leader's confidence will have a dramatic effect on the success of the ministry. Supervision is not dissecting people to find their weakness. Rather, it is enlarging their base of understanding and helping them move into more creative and responsive ministry.

Asking Permission

An important third step follows directly behind listening and identifying areas for growth. This is the step of asking permission. For instance, the supervisor may ask, "Would you like to work in this area?" The one being supervised has made a contract and in general has asked for help. Now the offer of help becomes more specific. The supervisor asks permission of the one being supervised in order to focus their efforts on agreed-upon areas. Perhaps the one being supervised says, "No, I'm not sure that this is the exact issue." Together the supervisor and the one being supervised define their areas of needed growth. This is supervision at its best.

Asking permission should not be overlooked. It is an important step that shows respect; it ensures that a person's dignity is not being violated. It communicates that the individual in ministry is in control. Asking permission lifts up the person. If the one being equipped for a ministry takes responsibility for growth, then learning becomes permanent. In fact, in such supervision, the supervisor may well admit that he or she needs to learn more in this area as well and that together they can learn and grow. To learn as a team is a significant step in establishing a solid supervisory relationship.

Asking permission and receiving consent frees the supervisor to go to work. It's "let us" rather than "you" or "me." It is "ours" rather than "yours" or "mine." Truly, if a ministry is shared, we are working together for its success, and we're helping one another grow in faith. Rather than trying to squeeze in his or her own thought or word of direction, the supervisor intentionally explores areas of growth with an individual. At first there may be certain areas that are off limits because of the confines of the agreement. However, as confidence develops in one area, the way often opens to even harder areas. Asking permission opens the process of growth that develops with time.

The yes, when it comes, is a confirmation that good supervision has been happening. Yes indicates receptivity, initiative, and response. Listening has been effective; timing has paid off. The yes is an invitation to enter deeper into the process, and one yes often leads to another yes. This approach helps persons take initiative to discover new growth areas. It even leads the supervisor into greater intentionality in the work of supervision.

The yes is ultimately a yes to God's initiative, which is leading all along the way to growth in ministry. Such is the case with Isaiah in his experience in the temple. Isaiah has a glimpse of God in all of God's splendor and might. That is enough to make him feel inadequate, and he says he is a man of unclean lips. Then comes the cleansing from God—and the challenge, "Whom shall I send, and who will go for us?" After working through his fears and seeing what the call would require, Isaiah responds, "Here am I! Send me" (Isaiah 6:8). If needed growth can be identified and help is rendered, persons in ministry will begin, like Isaiah, to feel more "sent," more self-confident, and more bold.

Discussing Resources

A fourth step in supervision is discussing available resources. Discovering resources becomes the responsibility of the one being supervised but is also an opportunity for the supervisor. As one begins to search for resources, new leads emerge. Names arise in articles; pieces are suggested in footnotes; workshops are advertised. Unhelpful books and articles need to be weeded out. Although discovering proper resources takes time and energy, it is an important skill to learn for growth in ministry. While energy is expended in discovering new and creative resources, the effort will pay great dividends in formation for ministry.

If the ministry is with young children, a helpful resource may need to focus on children of that age group and what needs they have.[3] If the ministry is feeding the homeless, a visit to a homeless shelter, with interviews with volunteers and organizers, could be an invaluable resource. Many videos are being created as resources for ministry.[4] Also one can check with religious bookstores as well as regional and denominational offices. Write to the staff of your own denomination's national office, which can usually serve as a helpful resource for the ministry one is attempting to accomplish. One does not have to operate in a vacuum to learn about ministry in general or about a specialized ministry in particular.

Discussing these resources can maximize the benefit drawn from them. Questions may be raised: "What are you discovering about your ministry in your reading?" "What did you find in terms of the growth areas in which you are working?" These kinds of questions draw us back to the objectives of the contract and the goals of the ministry, which include learning about ministry in general, about one's area in particular, and about one's own spiritual growth.

Supervision should have an educational component. Discussing resources can help provide new ideas that broaden one's vision of what is possible and offer something concrete to give shape to nebulous ideas and unclear dreams. Ideas found in resources can be copied, of course, but they can also spark new, creative thinking. The use of resources can help a ministry grow in depth and breadth.

Developing an Action Plan

The fifth area of supervision is helping a leader develop a plan of action. A person may share with the supervisor what plans have been emerging; the supervisor will listen and help discern what patterns have been developing in ministry. Then the supervisor can help that person clarify the possibilities under consideration and help her or him look ahead at the possible results of each course of action. The supervisor may also observe the comfort level felt by the leader with each option. Helpful feedback is not only in order but in most cases is expected and desired by the one being supervised.

This is also another good time for the supervisor to raise topics around the identified growth areas. For example, the supervisor may observe a similar negative pattern developing that has developed for the person in the past. Persons in ministry may be totally unaware that the situation in which they find themselves has similar dynamics to former experiences. If delegating has been a struggle, for instance, a reminder by the supervisor to delegate may be appropriate. Also, if progress is being observed in a person's goals, the supervisor can reinforce such growth with positive feedback.

As new avenues are explored in a ministry, the supervisor may suggest other alternatives. New options may be utilized; new ideas can be injected. Without becoming overbearing or recalling endless tales, the supervisor may say, "In my experience, I have found that this way works, but that way usually has a limited effect." Or the supervisor may say, "What would happen if you concentrated in this area and deemphasized that other area?" The supervisor can serve as a resource, highlighting options and helping the person anticipate probable consequences. Growth is set in the context of action.

Supervision calls for the best of planning. Often the supervisor can help a person break down desired growth into specific steps toward a goal. Establishing time lines, intermediate steps, and proper interventions are all appropriate. The supervisor helps a person in ministry continually evaluate what is happening with a ministry. The discussion can range from sharing how things are going to how an event fulfilled hoped-for objectives. What was achieved? What was learned? How can we build on the things that went right? How can we grow in ministry?

If patience was the issue originally identified in the example of working with young children, perhaps one could find kinship with Paul, who saw patience as one of the fruits of the spirit. Perhaps an action plan would include a time of centered prayer before teaching the class in order to become quiet within. The plan may include rearranging the room and using some opening exercise that the earlier children could engage in while others were arriving. We may look at things such as the level of one's voice—speaking more quietly when otherwise feeling exasperated and tempted to yell. If biblical knowledge is needed, perhaps one needs to enter a Bible study series so that the stories of the faith are more familiar. The action plan could then be to embark on a series of studies that coincide with the current Bible focus being used in ministry. In either case, the person could keep a journal both of discoveries of patience or of biblical truths.

Supervision should enable a leader to develop a plan of action. The supervisor becomes the needed helper to work out that course of action. This might mean trying one approach one time and another approach a different time and then comparing the two. Also, one may need to involve other persons or make special provision for avoiding an unwanted situation. Contingency plans are often lifesavers when other plans do not work out. The supervisor can help a person keep on track in the growth areas of ministry and can help work through the rough spots, but the supervisor is not responsible for rescuing a ministry if all seems to be going wrong.

Good supervision helps the ministry gain momentum, which ensures progress, growth, and spiritual awareness. Growing in spiritual awareness can be tracked by asking such questions as: "Is one coming to depend more and more on God's strength?" "Is one finding that one's talents are growing as invested in the kingdom?" "Are relationships becoming more wholesome?" "Is one's sense of appreciation for life and God's gifts growing?" Developing a positive course of action means we are growing spiritually.

Modeling

The sixth area of supervising is modeling. Of course, a supervisor does not announce that he or she is going to model what a person should become for others. However, this is in fact what a supervisor should be doing, and the more aware one is of it, the more intentionally such modeling can take place. Example is indeed the best teacher. The one being supervised certainly needs to learn to listen; to support another individual; to help identify growth areas; to set up and facilitate a program; and to learn about themselves, others, and God. The supervisor provides a positive pattern that has application for ministry.

Modeling is important because the supervisor is an example of the merger of belief and practice. What one is becomes just as important as what one does. If the one being supervised believes in the authenticity of the supervisor, then the process will be a powerful influence in a person's formation in ministry. In fact, religious formation in general may be at its height in training for ministry. Modeling should therefore be a self-conscious aspect of the supervisor's work.

The topic of what ministry means may emerge directly as the one being supervised asks why the supervisor is making particular suggestions. This is a marvelous opportunity to explore why certain choices are made. Doubts may be raised and questions asked. The supervisor must be prepared to identify with the struggles in ministry and explore how these are handled. This dialogue can be invaluable. Questions raised in supervision can also be helpful for the supervisor. All concerns are openings to share in the nature, calling, and purpose of ministry. The supervisor can share why choices are made in the light of merging one's beliefs with practical application. Here teaching of beliefs is done, and a spirit is set for personal and congregational growth.

The best preparation for the role of modeling is to keep growing in one's own ministry as a supervisor. The supervisor sets the pace. The supervisor will be handling the frustrations, ambiguities, and tough decisions that come with ministry. By handling these in a constructive manner, the supervisor signals that ministry is an intentional vocation. The supervisor keeps stretching and growing. The practitioner in ministry is the teacher of ministry. Renewal of one's ministry becomes merged with being spiritually alive.

Growing Spiritually

The ministry supervisor should have the willingness and readiness to lift up the spiritual dynamics of ministry as they arise and to relate them to particular areas of implementing a ministry. Persons being supervised may need to work through an entirely new area in their spiritual development as they see others growing or asking questions. The supervisor can point to areas where God's grace is real and to spiritual resources for developing disciplines of faith adequate to the calling of ministry. The supervisor should attempt to relate to others in a way that maintains a full awareness of the person of Christ. Spiritual awareness should not be an afterthought but rather an integral part of each area of supervision.

Therefore, development of the spiritual life of the supervisor is important. Only a life rooted in in-depth prayer will have the awareness needed for supervision in ministry.[5] Continual opening to the Living Presence is the resource that will yield the creative responses needed in supervision. A regular discipline of Bible study will result in a biblical awareness that is constantly informing the supervision process. Prayer is also a natural part of such a discipline. Prayer is developing an attentiveness to God, listening to the voice of the loving presence of Christ, and seeking the leading of the Holy Spirit. Keeping a prayer journal could well be part of such a discipline. Spiritual awareness results in a peace that enhances the very relationship the supervisor has with the one being supervised. Being spiritually alert will keep the supervisor attuned to the spiritual needs of the one being supervised as well as of those served in the ministry at hand. The love of God discovered by the supervisor is passed on in the style of supervision that points toward the growth of God's kingdom.[6]

The supervisor demonstrates values that are being implemented in ministry. By pointing to dynamics of faith, the supervisor helps open up spiritual awareness and points toward growth. A ministry becomes truly exciting when, through good supervision, persons keep attuned to their growing sense of faith in God. Authenticity of ministry comes as one uses one's beliefs to respond as Christ's servant in each opportunity. If the style of the servant leader shows through, then a person's spiritual awareness is turned into a real ministry. Growing spiritually makes supervision a ministry of God's presence. Strength from God become real.

Outcomes

The outcomes of supervision for ministry are many. Supervision helps persons feel they are accomplishing something and that they are growing. Individuals are no longer reluctant to take on a position because they know they will not be abandoned but will rather receive the help they need to accomplish a new endeavor. The supervisory relationship becomes cherished. Even after the formal sessions of supervision are over, persons know where they can turn for help. A relationship is established. Rather than a hit-or-miss practice, ministry becomes intentional and focused. The entire church benefits because persons know that a well-thought-out plan is in operation.

The results of supervision speak directly to issues raised in such resources as *How to Prevent Lay Leader Burnout*[7] and *The Care and Feeding of Volunteers.*[8] Inadequate task descriptions often result in persons feeling inadequately trained to do tasks at hand and realizing what a big responsibility they have taken upon themselves. The causes of burnout are best offset early by helping volunteers plan and grow in specific ways. A supervision process is an open channel of communication that helps persons grow into their work and feel a real sense of appreciation for what they have to offer. A positive tone is established. A healthy and joyful spirit spreads.[9]

A cadre of leaders is in training. Because this training is spiritually oriented, a lot of excitement is generated as spiritual themes come alive and persons grow in ministry. A church that takes training and supervision seriously makes a long-term investment. Leaders trained in one area may apply skills years later to another area in the church. When training and supervision are involved, there is always a sense of growth and excitement. New arenas of service are opening, and growth is occurring. Supervision helps define courses of permanent growth in ministry. We can celebrate the investment that persons make not only to do a good job but to grow in faith and to help others do the same. A new heart and new spirit are in formation.

Chapter 6

Covenanting for Renewal

So far we have been speaking about establishing and implementing a process of renewal. We have seen how the biblical call of unbinding can help a church find a new heart and new spirit. We have matched strengths with needs, set goals and time lines, and even discussed how training and supervision can help a plan of renewal come to fruition. Is that not enough?

Yes—and no. A lot of good will certainly be done if we get this far. However, to come to its fullest fruition, any renewal in the church needs continual nurturing. In this chapter we will step back a bit to see how to further shape and fashion the process of renewal—like a sculptor putting the finishing touches on a piece of art.

We call this "covenanting for renewal," since members of the church in renewal unite themselves with Christ and with one another in response to God's calling. Like the experience of the Israelites who came through the Red Sea to Mount Sinai, where they made a covenant with God and one another, so these processes form and shape us as the people of God. This was the hope of God as expressed by Ezekiel: "I will be their God, and they shall be my people" (Ezekiel 37:27). We speak in covenantal language since the church is fashioned as a people in Christ, bound together in his love. Such unbinding brings new life. A new heart and a new spirit are more than program and budget and ministries, although each is needed. A soul, a spiritual vitality, must also emerge. Let us consider how this new life is nurtured.

Encouraging Renewal

Background and Rationale

For renewal to occur in a congregation, encouragement is needed from many people. The life of unbinding is a new and different experience, and persons face concerns as new life comes forth. Most are going to feel tentative at first. Are we capable of this? Will all this work? What might happen if new members come into the church or new classes are formed or old-timers discover new life? In fact, what will *I* be like if *I* am renewed? We know that biblical love casts out fear and, a lot of tender loving care is needed to encourage renewal.

In fact, regular encouragement is essential in a church renewal project. Remember how the people of Israel wandered so long in the wilderness? Even when their goal became clear, they had to deal with many disappointments on their way to the land of milk and honey. Christian growth requires patience during the rough moments. Remembering that God is reaching out in these rough moments can be enough to help persons move on, turning difficulties into learning experiences rather than defeats.

The leadership of the church needs to offer ongoing support throughout the renewal process. Those who originally identified strengths of the congregation should continue to provide encouragement as new growth comes forth. Even if others' experiences differ from their own, leaders can identify with the enthusiasm of renewal and help deal with the disappointments. In order not to react to difficulties or to the fear that things are returning to the status quo, leaders must continuously operate out of their sense of vision and hope.

Step Toward Renewal #14

The renewal committee considers how to offset fears of renewal with encouragement and support and how to address any specific concerns.

Renewal needs to be shaped and fashioned. Like the artist, those in renewal form and shape the contours of growth in a positive, encouraging style. While some fears are general in nature, others are quite specific. If fears are addressed in a loving manner, trust and hope can grow. The renewal committee should spend time together in prayer for leaders old and new, for each other, and for the church's ministries. Members should then discuss how to encourage each person who has taken on new leadership responsibilities. Other concerns can be discussed and resources rallied to keep the renewal effort moving toward completion of the stated objectives. The renewal committee can identify times when persons need rest and times when celebration can affirm growth. Gentle shaping is a must for renewal to continue.

When the Christian education program in one renewal project came alive, the children began asking a lot more questions about why the church does what it does. The fifth and sixth graders began studying the "ordinances," the sacraments of the church. In this church's tradition the Eucharist is observed with a Love Feast meal of beef and bread. In their discussion the young people wondered why hamburgers could not be served instead. Several youngsters were very vocal. Rather than squash what was resulting from enthusiasm and interest in the church, the teachers decided to take the consideration to the deacons. At this point the deacons could have refused to consider the untraditional request, but they were wise enough to do otherwise. They discussed the entire matter with the young people and commended them for so thoughtfully considering the practices of the church. They told the fifth and sixth graders that hamburgers would be fine since the meal was a symbol of the love among believers; the menu was secondary, although beef was probably easier to prepare. The youth were tickled that their proposal was so thoughtfully considered. Although they soon agreed that hamburgers would be a lot of work, they concluded that partaking of hamburgers would be their preferred way of celebrating their love for each other. As a result of dialogue and encouragement, a valuable lesson on the purpose of communion was learned, and new life was fostered.

As church walls are pushed outward, new kinds of questions will be asked. New questions do not have to be a threat; they are signs of renewal. New questions indicate interest that needs to be encouraged and properly channeled. Encouraging the positive is an effective and genuine methodology for bringing forth new life. Within that perspective, what does not work well can be addressed in love. The spirit of the whole endeavor becomes a crucial part of the renewal project.

Words spoken at church board meetings can lift up and encourage new life rather than just be "reports." Time can be set aside to sign letters of encouragement. Encouragement can be offered by including a project or an outgrowth of a ministry (such as a life-sized figure of Paul from the youth club) in the Sunday morning worship service. Encouragement can come by highlighting exciting moments of a ministry in the monthly newsletter or weekly bulletin. Encouragement can be offered in a card or a note; postcards are a wonderful tool for this purpose and can be easily purchased and carried for use when waiting for a plane or a meeting. Encouragement is an essential ingredient in renewal.

Outcomes

As encouragement is given, a congregation begins to feel good about itself. Individuals begin to feel that they can accomplish something. Reports become reoriented toward what has been accomplished and what needs to be accomplished. Frustrating meetings lessen, and communication increases. Persons may begin to note that they are surprising even themselves in what they are capable of doing. In some cases new jealousies may arise momentarily, but as each person finds a spot to fit in, such feelings can be overcome. With encouragement, persons will find the strength to make it over the hurdles and will discover new arenas for growth.

Another outcome of encouragement is helping leaders focus on what needs to be done. Rather than leaving a ministry on its own, leaders do a lot to guide a project by expressing encouragement. Encouragement is more than just saying, "You're doing a good job." It means listening deeply to the struggles of others and lifting up the themes that help move a ministry along. Encouragement keeps everyone focused on all that is hoped for, even when roadblocks are encountered along the way. Support helps persons keep aware of the bigger picture. In reality, such encouragement may well be what keeps a ministry going at the crucial moments when despair could set in. Encouragement also gives persons permission to celebrate the gains as they come—and keeps growth happening during the ups and downs that naturally come.

Understanding Growth

Background and Rationale

Martin Saarinen, in his monograph on "The Life Cycle of a Congregation,"[1] looks at the development of a congregation in terms of the "gene structures" of the church. For Saarinen, there are four genes. *E* stands for

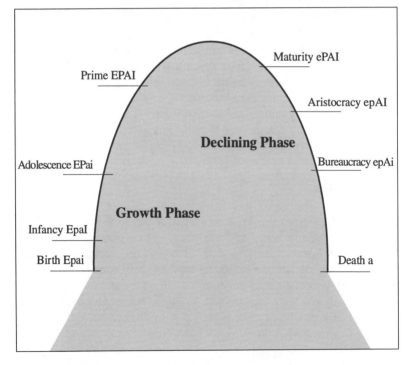

energy or the energizing function, that which gets the congregation going; the energy can emerge from a leader or a movement. P stands for programs—those services that respond to the needs of a congregation, the ministries, the functions. Unlike E, which is internal, P is the externals. A stands for administration—goals and budgets and plans. Administration is the harmonizing function where things are drawn together in a common purpose and the resources gathered to accomplish them. Finally, I stands for inclusion and relates to how persons are drawn in and assimilated. How are gifts being used? How is conflict being handled?[2]

Saarinen helps us picture the growth and renewal of a congregation by observing stages from birth, infancy, adolescence, and prime to maturity, aristocracy, bureaucracy, and death. The up side of the cycle begins with birth, where there is big E and small p, a, and i. We see this as high enthusiasm and energy. At this stage there is undifferentiated energy, E. Infancy comes as the inclusion function, I, grows and persons are invited in. There is openness and welcome. Adolescence sees the growth of program, the focusing of efforts on meeting of needs. P increases. However, one factor already comes into question, that is of inclusion, the I factor. Saarinen finds (and don't we all) that the requirements of programs and services can come at the expense of people's needs. Herein decline may already be in the offing. For Saarinen the prime is when a heightened A is added so that people concerns can be balanced with program concerns, and mission is lifted up.

Saarinen helps us look at the development of a program or of general renewal in the church. Renewal occurs as all four "genes" are kept in a dynamic relationship. Certainly everyone experiences the way people get left out when program needs overtake people needs. Saarinen shows us that the cycle of growth can be reawakened by going back to discover basic mission and purpose.[3] This is our E. Saarinen relies on the concept of servanthood, which he says "impels the congregation to be aware of the many forms of ministry in which its members participate in church and society, to assess the gifts given by the Spirit to the congregation for ministry, and to account for their use."[4] A new heart and a new spirit can be discovered by calling forth the ministries. "Unbind him and let him go," Jesus said of Lazarus—lest death overtake us.

The seed of decline, according to Saarinen, is right within each factor for growth. Diminished energy, e, is usually the first to decline as a congregation enters maturity. The vision and excitement that called the church into being begins to wane. Next to decline is program, p, as fewer people attend and the debate comes in "who's in" and "who's out." Preserving the status quo is important. Next to go is inclusion, i, as the church enters bureaucracy. Structures remain, but high boundaries guard the terrain. Finally the administrative structures go, a. At this point, intervention is crucial. Energy needs to be rediscovered and a vision regained or death occurs. Inclusion needs to be lifted up. New programs that speak to the needs of people must be identified. For Saarinen, the possibility for renewal is related to the level of crisis in the congregation. By rediscovering its vision and its setting, new life can come forth.

Step Toward Renewal #15

As a renewal committee, spend time assessing the congregation's points of growth and the vital balance of the components of church renewal.

Actually, at any point along the way, the renewal committee can step back and look at the overview of church renewal. Energy is a major issue. Persons wonder how a congregation can discover or rediscover vitality. What makes for spiritual growth? What has been the vision and dynamic force of a congregation? What strengths are inherent and given by God? As Saarinen notes, the potential for new energy is related to the level of crisis. New energy is found by recapturing the church's historic vision and rediscovering the "mandate for ministry" in its current setting. A reawakened sense of mission can occur with intentional rediscovery of new birth.[5] The renewal committee can well consider the implications of such themes and explore steps for action in order to nurture the renewal of the congregation.

In guiding renewal, we can see how important it is to keep each aspect of the life of a congregation in balance. Just as program needs must be balanced with people needs, administration is important and does not have to be a "necessary evil." The coordinating function of administration is crucial for the mission to be accomplished. The supervisory function outlined in this resource is a dynamic part of administration. Herein people resources are enhanced and utilized. Through servant leadership, the renewal committee can sense what needs should be addressed and how to rally the resources.

In the middle of renewal at Bush Creek, one of the key leaders was signaling a need for a rest. How would we make it without this person? At first we were a bit frightened. Would everything collapse? However, the need for her to rest and "be fallow" was affirmed. The board enlisted two persons to take this woman's spot. What happened amazed us all. First, she got her needed rest—and had the chance to reconnect with other adults and grow personally. Secondly, the persons who took the vacated spot found they grew in ways they never imagined and discovered that they could actually do what they had felt incapable of doing. Finally, the committee in charge decided to establish a rotation pattern in order to give anyone who needed it the chance to recharge. Energy increased rather than decreased all the way around. By keeping its ear to the ground, leadership saved the day. The vital balance was maintained between serving program needs and people needs. Keeping the needs of people and the growth of members a priority can help the congregation respond to the new life that comes forth.

A congregation that has begun the renewal process will want renewal to be an ongoing process for the church. If a church is two years into its plan of renewal, for instance, it will want to begin thinking about the next three years beyond the current plan. For that purpose, it can start planning another congregational meeting to assess its current strengths. Part of such a gathering may include evaluation of the process thus far and further charting of the course for the future. However, the main focus of the meeting should be to affirm strengths. Some new ones may well emerge that did not exist three years ago. The church can look toward setting a second three-year plan of renewal that builds on the first three years.

Outcomes

A major outcome of the renewal committee assessing growth is to understand where the church is in the cycle of renewal. Such "aha!" moments can be crucial as a church identifies the factors that have been at work in growth and decline. By finding itself in the continuum of renewal, a congregation discovers where it is in the cycle of growth and decline. Self-understanding can free it from being stymied by the prevailing forces and can release it from the paralysis of factors that cause decline. When a church sees that new energy is the needed factor, it can spend time regaining its purpose from the past or exploring its calling from its context in the present. In a similar way, a congregation can discover that people concerns must be balanced with program concerns, that inclusion factors are important for growth, that a church can take positive steps toward renewal. A congregation can benefit from positive reflection on its situation and its calling for ministry.

In stepping back from the process, a church can gain a perspective on its history and begin a healthy, ongoing, lifelong process of intentional renewal. Rather than just responding to immediate needs and crises, the church begins to chart a course toward the future. One church leader I knew claimed that ten years is needed to start up any significant project. This accounts for all the stages of growth and development, as well as for solidifying one's vision in response to changing needs. The plan of renewal as established in this resource could well be used to set up such a ten-year plan. Take a year to set up a three-year plan of renewal for your church. At the beginning of the third year of implementation, hold another meeting (or series of meetings) to identify new strengths and formulate a second three-year plan. Repeat the process again at the beginning of the third year of the second three-year plan. In this manner, a church can project an initial year of planning followed by three three-year plans of renewal. Some of the subsequent plans may be, of course, to continue what is already started. However, the church can also put into place some ministries that will need to wait until other priorities have been accomplished. Crucial will be its assimilation process of members, the topic to which we now turn.

Assimilating New Members

Background and Rationale

We can see how assimilating new members is a key part of the process of church renewal. Some will already be present in a church's life but have not yet found a place to fit in. Others will be either friends of church members or strangers who show up at a church event. Some will inquire about the church over the telephone.

People are not automatically assimilated. Often they come in the front door and go out the back door. An entire process of incorporating them is entailed, from the point of searching to the initial inquiry to a person taking the initial steps of discipleship.[6] For inclusion to happen in the church, attention must be given to this important part of the renewal of a congregation, and everyone plays a vital part in the assimilation of both new and old members.

Inactive members are a real concern to many in the church. Just as in caring for our physical bodies preventative medicine is the best approach, so we can anticipate ways to build healthy and growing spiritual church bodies. The renewal committee has already been discussing the materials available to help persons grow in faith. It must also look at how persons find their way into the church initially and then into a deeper life of discipleship. How do new persons come into the inner circles? How do long-term members keep their faith alive and become more assimilated? In successful assimilation, persons move from needing to feel invited themselves to taking responsibility for inviting others.[7]

Step Toward Renewal #16

The renewal committee looks at the entire assimilation process and explores ways for persons to become part of the life of the congregation.

Materials about assimilating new members abound. In a helpful book by that very title, *Assimilating New Members,*[8] Lyle Schaller comes at the question by exploring ways a local congregation *excludes* members. In fact, he list twelve ways to keep people from joining a church, including for instance, "Don't invite them." As Schaller notes, some persons assume they aren't welcome unless invited. The renewal committee could begin by looking at how "welcoming" is accomplished or not accomplished. By putting themselves in the shoes of a newcomer who drives by the building, looking for parking, and enters the church doors, the renewal committee can explore what steps should be taken for extending better hospitality to a newcomer. We can learn much about renewal by discussing how persons find their way physically and spiritually into the church and which obstacles might deter entry.

In a striking article in *Christian Century,* Gene and Nancy Preston tell of their frustration in trying to find a friendly church.[9] Settling into an East Coast college town known for its quality of life, they began to go church hunting. They visited ten mainline congregations, returned to three congregations twice, and visited a Roman Catholic parish. They arrived early to services, signed the guest registry, and stayed for the post-service fellowship. At the latter, they noted that friends often tried to catch up with one another. As visitors, they were left alone. While they received some nice form letters, not even one of the twenty-four ordained staff of the churches phoned them. None of their neighbors, who attended some of these churches they had visited, extended an invitation for them to return. Such an experience of one family clues us in to the desperate need for churches to welcome newcomers and assimilate new members.

The Prestons offered some recommendations for churches that a renewal committee would do well to consider. For instance, make sure your signs are readable to people in moving cars and that they are inviting. In the registry have a place not only to check for the pastor to call but for a layperson to call—and then follow through! The Prestons recommend that pastors be a lot more available to newcomers on Sunday morning and put hospitality ahead of church business. They recommend congregations consider the purpose of the coffee fellowship. If greeting newcomers is one of the purposes, how can discussion be stimulated to include new persons? Interestingly, the Prestons also recommend that the social skills of older members be used to help newcomers feel at home because they found that those over sixty-five had the social confidence to help them as strangers. Each of their recommendations could help the renewal committee train the congregation to reach out to new people.

Outcomes

By taking the above steps, the assimilation of new members becomes an intentional rather than a hit-or-miss process. If the Great Commission is our mandate, then welcoming new members is part and parcel to our mission. After being welcomed, persons then need to be led into a deeper faith journey. The results of assimilation will ultimately be that persons become growing, responding Christians who find a way to put their faith into practice.

Considering the assimilation process helps the entire congregation develop a healthier life. Persons become more sensitive to one another, expanding their fellowship circles to include and invite others in the congregation to special events. New persons then begin to find their way into the church. Focusing on assimilating persons also helps keep members from becoming inactive. By continually building up the body, persons become attuned to one another. They also experience the great reward of deepening one's own spiritual life by reaching out to others.

Assimilating new members correlates with keeping old members. Like a marriage, the relationship of members to their church never remains static. Either it is growing deeper or it is deteriorating. As a church begins to grow, it is important that long-standing members find new challenges for growth. It doesn't help for them simply to turn over tasks to newcomers. In fact, we learned at Bush Creek that newcomers did not want that kind of process; they needed the experience of the long-term members. The renewal process requires that all persons be artfully integrated into new areas of growth. Longer-term members can serve on teams with new persons or act as advisors. Serving on the renewal committee itself would be a way for long-standing members to find a new challenge of service.

Renewing and Serving

Background and Rationale

Lest we get the impression that all this renewing is self-serving, we need to note that serving is integral to covenanting of renewal. Each of the church renewal projects that informed this handbook had a service motif. The plan for ministry had a mission-and-service component. Besides the clothing room that was developed for the neighborhood, a host of other programs emerged, from persons collecting donations in soup cans to help combat world hunger to individuals taking meals to someone going through a difficult time. In the transformational Sunday school project, exchanges were held between children's classes in rural Lancaster County and inner-city Philadelphia. "CROP walk for the hungry" signs were prominent in another church where a large Sunday school was involved. Some members of one of the churches that was building more room for adult Sunday School classes took off work to hammer thousands of roofing nails, not to reduce the building loan but to give the savings to the world's hungry. The Alban Institute project noted that social service ministries often accompanied the contextual elements of the sixteen growing churches it studied. Clearly, growing churches had outreach into their communities and the world.[10]

Step Toward Renewal #17

The renewal committee gathers suggestions for meaningful service projects so that members can have options for making service a part of their journey of faith.

Some types of service projects will fit more appropriately than others. Some will have an evangelistic or mission orientation; others will have more of a community-building focus. Some projects are close at hand, lending themselves to on-site visits or work; other projects involve travel, even to remote regions of the world. Ideas for appropriate service projects may grow out of a group's study or a special contact. A good service project becomes integral to the life of a congregation. In fact, working together on it can form lifelong bonds. Persons often maintain interest in those projects for years to come and pass the stories and interest on to others, including their children.

Outcomes

In serving we discover what kind of community we want to be. Many people of God in Scripture were service-oriented. Be it by evangelizing in a worldwide mission outreach or by meeting the human needs right in our neighborhood, the gospel is always directed both inward and outward. Serving helps us look beyond ourselves. It helps keep before us the gospel mandate to feed the hungry and clothe the naked. A deeper covenant with God is formed within as we grow in love and service to those around us, and some special bonding happens between people as they are serving and being served. As a tree is known by the fruit it bears, so a church shows its renewed love by the fruits of its service and outreach.

As a result, much is accomplished for Christ and the church. Many small efforts help meet the human needs of our communities, our nation, and our world. The long-term outcomes of projects like Habitat for Humanity, CROP, the Heifer Project, and Church World Service are many. While needs are great, the effects of the gospel are multiplied when loving service is faithfully applied. The gospel directs us to the hungry, the homeless, and the disinherited. We know that in serving the least of these, we serve Christ. Service is a real mark of renewal, and Christ's presence is experienced as we share in his ministry of compassion.

Chapter 7

The Church in Transformation

In this chapter we will explore the transformation process in greater depth. First we'll look at transformation from the biblical perspective of Psalm 51. Then we'll see the exciting results of some of the churches who followed the renewal plan outlined in this book. In Chapter 8, we'll consider some dynamics of renewal.

The transformation of renewal means new life is coming into being in the church. Growth is occurring. What has been binding life is cut loose. The grave cloths are removed as forms of death are imbued with new life. Who says things can't change? Who says there is no hope? Transforming the church *is* possible. God wills vitality and growth in persons and in the corporate body. God creates a new heart and a new spirit.

Creating a New Heart and a New Spirit

"Create in me a clean heart, O God, and put a new and right spirit within me," pleads the psalmist (Psalm 51:10). The vision that Ezekiel asserted for the nation (Ezekiel 11:17ff; 36:24ff) the psalmist pictured as possible for the individual. God delivers people; God creates a new heart and a new spirit. The psalmist points to the depth and scope of transformation as the struggles of the human heart are brought before God. Psalm 51 is a psalm for renewal of the very center of the religious life of God's people. Though sometimes dated earlier, Psalm 51 actually has references to the deliverance of the Israelites and the restoration of the temple: "Do good to Zion in thy good pleasure; rebuild the walls of Jerusalem" (v. 18). In his distress the psalmist turns upward to God and discovers an unfolding of faith that changes his mood and approach.

This psalm suggests a threefold movement of renewal that has both personal and corporate implications: upward, inward, and outward. In the midst of our desire for renewal, we turn upward to God, who creates within us a new heart and a new spirit that spells an outward joy and thanksgiving. A transformation occurs. In this section, we will look at the first of the two movements in the psalm in order to find the depth and scope of renewal: first upward, and then inward.

The psalm begins with a prayer for deliverance: "Have mercy on me, O God, according to thy steadfast love" (v. 1). From his point of critical need, the psalmist cries out for help. He depends on God for love. In this first of the so-called penitential psalms, the author does not recount why God should love him or what he has done in the past to merit receiving such love. In utter desperation he cries out, declaring that he is wholly dependent on God for everything.[1] Showing his abiding trust in God, the psalmist acknowledges that through turning upward to God, he can find renewal. Renewal spells a restored relationship to God.

The first step of renewal is therefore to turn upward to God. Recognizing our need for renewal is actually a statement that we are not helpless. By turning to God, we claim that more is possible.[2] Transformation can occur. In affirming the majesty of God in the midst of our despair, we claim the first movement of renewal. God through love demonstrated in Christ Jesus reaches out to us. Renewal speaks of God's action of transformation. As the apostle Paul so often speaks of putting off the old and putting on the new, so renewal is the gift of the transforming power of God claimed as possible and real. New life can be ours.

In a helpful booklet, *Dynamics of Renewal: A Biblical Study,* Manfred Brauch says, "The verb 'renew' and the noun 'renewal' have the literal sense 'to make new again.' "[3] This is in keeping with the Old Testament understanding of God's renewing activity. God's spirit makes new. In referring to 2 Corinthians 4:16, where Paul speaks of "being renewed everyday," Brauch points out how in the midst of greatest difficulty we discover the certainty of two truths: "One, that our mortality will be overcome in the resurrection (4:14), and two, that already in the present, God is powerfully present (4:7) and working a deep, inner renewal (4:16)."[4] Recognizing our need happens in the same breath as affirming our possibilities. This is our first step in renewal, the upward turn.

Renewal begins as we turn to God and rediscover the source of our life. Then we can begin to rediscover our energy. As we noted earlier, in the analysis of the life cycle of a congregation, only as a people rediscover their energy can growth and renewal occur. Looking upward to God, a church can get in touch with its mandate for ministry. "Together, a reawakened sense of those forces which had previously breathed life into the congregation and an adequate perception of the possibilities for ministry in the congregation and community may combine to produce the condition whereby the congregation can continue to participate in the representation of Christ in that place in some new way."[5] In the midst of his distress, the psalmist reaches his hands toward God, and that is the beginning of change. Out of a felt need for renewal, a congregation can take its first step by turning upward to God.

This upward turn is followed by an inward exploration. In the midst of this felt need, the psalmist points us to renewal. "Create in me a clean heart, O God, and put a new and right spirit within me." The psalmist yearns for an inner transformation. In the context of the psalm, we see just what a new heart means. The psalmist is yearning for God and wants his whole being to be turned toward God. Biblically the heart is the "point of contact with God." "The heart, as the innermost spring of the human personality, is directly open to God and subject to his influence."[6] A new heart means a new orientation.

For the psalmist this is discovered in secret: "Behold, thou desirest truth in the inward being; therefore teach me wisdom in my secret heart" (v. 6). His earnest meditation before God in his heart (in secret) is the place where God himself reveals to the worshiper how everything ultimately holds together (the poet, like Paul in Romans 11:33, calls it 'wisdom').[7] Wisdom means one's very way of living emerges out of one's inner relationship with God. Like the Book of James in the New Testament, there is a quiet understanding that one's outer life, even through times of distress, is guided by an inner relationship with Christ Jesus.[8] A new heart, a special inner discovery of faith, is affirmed.

In church renewal, much of the practical way is found from that discovery of God within the heart. In servant leadership, the servant listens. The leader of renewal listens to the heart both to discover God's presence as well as to find the practical way of renewal. Focusing on the heart, persons can discover God's living presence and discern how their call is central to new life in the church.[9] As the practical examples of churches illustrate below, the entire congregation is led into these secret discoveries in the process of renewal. Teamwork is developed as a congregation explores how the Holy Spirit is speaking in the heart. The very presence of God enriches, empowers, and leads along the way.

Just as there is a new heart, so there is a new spirit. From Psalm 51 the author envisions a union with God that is dynamic rather than static. "Cast me not away from thy presence, and take not thy holy Spirit from me. Restore to me the joy of thy salvation, and uphold me with a willing spirit" (vv. 11-12). There is a power and joy within that begins to cleanse and motivate. The discovery is one that faith is not lived out of the "ought" but in response to God's initiative. A new heart is matched with a new spirit where faith is a willing response to the new life God has in store.[10] Such faith is shared out of a living sense of God's leading within.

So much in renewal depends on the spirit of a congregation. This is the vitality and joy that is felt by someone who enters the congregation. Though they may not yet know where they fit in, newcomers can tell that something vibrant is happening. In the videotape of the Alban Institute study of growing churches, Roy Oswald relates how persons who come to such a church want to be a part; something is happening here in which people want to participate.[11] The spirit of a people is crucial for renewal. The sense of willingness of the new spirit is the gift of union with God that genuinely shines forth. Whether one is a lifelong member or a newcomer to a church, that spirit invites and sustains. That something special called renewal is not elusive; it is God's gift of a new heart and a new spirit.

Before exploring the third movement outward, in joy and thanksgiving, let us look at the results of these first two movements—upward and inward—in some of the churches that went through the process of renewal elaborated in this resource.

Renewal in the Churches

The three churches who entered the renewal process described in this handbook have exciting stories to tell. We will delineate the plan of renewal as described in the words of their pastors and then relate the outcomes of implementation to this point in time. None of these churches is an end product, to be sure, for renewal is still in process. Hints of new life serve as models for us. Each church needs to discover its own plan of renewal, given its unique calling, strengths, and needs. The joy that results, however, is common with each. We celebrate the signs of the kingdom we see in the examples of these churches.

Mayfair Conwell

In the Mayfair Conwell Church it was Pastor Marcia Bailey's deep conviction that "renewal isn't really about gaining new members; it is about experiencing the dynamic, empowering love and grace of God for oneself. It is about regaining excitement in faith; it's about allowing the Spirit to challenge anew." She and her congregation feel that preaching is a very effective tool for them, and so they turned to the Scriptures to find their call for renewal. Marcia designed a six-week series of services on renewal, using texts of asking for and receiving the indwelling of the Holy Spirit, looking into the mission and purpose of the church, and exploring the practical dimensions of Christian discipleship. Their key text was Numbers 11:4-30, where Moses, feeling the heavy responsibility of being the leader, gathers together seventy elders. However, the hope of Moses is beyond that. "Would that all the LORD's people were prophets, that the LORD would put his spirit upon them!" (Numbers 11:29).

The second part of the plan was for the pastor to lead the church council, made up of all officers and board members, to consider a six-hour planning retreat focused on envisioning, dreaming, and becoming. There they would be invited to review the past five years and reflect on the events, seasons, and occasions when they felt growth and excitement taking place. They would also be asked to reflect on the times when they did not. Following the premise that even the church cannot be all things to all people, especially the small church, the church would be challenged to discover their strengths, affirm their faithful work, and begin to envision new possibilities that might grow out of their corporate life. The pastor's hope was that the church would begin to see itself in a new, more positive light, thereby gaining insight and renewed hope.

The third step toward renewal was initiated simultaneously with the planning of the preaching and leadership retreat. The pastor suggested to the diaconate that within the year the church should have its first spiritual life retreat, which had previously been done only with the youth. A specific time away from daily routines and responsibilities would offer refreshment and opportunity to examine one's life and faith. The pastor felt that the church needed to program intentional time for spiritual renewal in order to strengthen the ones who served as a strength for others. She felt these three major components would "get us off the ground."

The results were many—and went beyond what was anticipated. The preaching series, aimed directly at personal renewal, generated much discussion and response within the congregation. In a somewhat humbling but effective fashion, the pastor related how she herself needed renewal. She brought a potted tree from her office into the Sunday worship service. The tree, she said, has tiny leaves that open and close like petals on a delicate flower, and its bright, vibrant color and gentle movements create a feeling of freshness, serenity, and peace. She shared how it was full of life and promise and hope. It had weathered storms of erratic watering and had survived cool winters and sweltering summers. The plant is committed to life and strength and growth. This tree is full of promises and possibilities.

Pastor Bailey went on to describe how this tree was much like our lives: "This is my tree, full of all those promises and possibilities I described— or is it? This is my tree. Does it look familiar? I ask not have you seen it before, because many of you have. But does it look familiar? Does it look like you? like you feel? like you are? Does it look like your spiritual life? Does it look like your devotional life? Does it look like your family life? Does it look like your marital life? Does it look like our church? This is my tree—green and leafy. Or is it dead and dying? Does it look like *you?* Does it look like *me?*"

Marcia went on to relate how she had enrolled in the course on church renewal. After juggling all the children, schedules, and driving, she got to her first class, only to have a sinking feeling that she had been there before. Six years ago, as a seminary student, she had taken the very same course. Should she go on? Should she drop the course? Should she tell the church that she had already taken it? She continued, "I knew then that I was like that tree that stands in my office. If anyone needed renewal, it was me. Do you ever feel like that? Like this is all a rerun, that you've been here before? Like things are familiar—too familiar, even boring, and you long for a sense that life is fresh, alive, and new?"

Returning to the biblical text, she shared how the Israelites felt that way. Freed from bondage in Egypt, they were headed for the Promised Land. However, life had gotten dull; things were pretty routine. Even the manna God provided for their daily food had a sameness to it, and they began to grumble, to be restless, to be discouraged, and to be discontented. As believers, Pastor Bailey noted, we can get the same way as our faith becomes mundane and all the excitement and vitality of belief seems to elude us. "We get that way as the church when we get comfortable and settled in our patterns, so comfortable that we forget to invite and include others. We forget our living, dynamic faith." Moses calls on God: "We need help. You must do something. If you can't change this, then take my life"—that's how discouraged he'd become. And God *does* do something; God tells Moses to gather seventy elders, and God places his spirit upon them, and they prophesy and are filled with encouragement, life, and God's message. In turn Moses pleads that all the Lord's people would be prophets and receive God's spirit.

"Would that the Lord's Spirit be on *us*," she preached, "we who like this plant are weary and lifeless and on the verge of death! God's Holy Spirit, living in us, giving us peace and comfort, yes, but also energizing us with dynamic vitality, promise and hope, and renewal and newness of life." Marcia shared how she went back to class, still uncertain whether to drop out or continue. Following that she had a meeting that didn't go as planned. By Wednesday, she prayed that God's Spirit would do something, grant life and hope. Then it happened. "Quietly God's Spirit began to work, nudging, stirring, moving, weaving around my discouragement, and granting me an inward peace." She shared how she learned again that renewal must first begin within each of us—"not by our actions but by God's action, by the indwelling presence of God's Holy Spirit, revitalizing, reenergizing, reviving all of us who get discouraged, weary, complacent, and sad. . . . In my office is a tree. It may look from where you are sitting to be dead, but if you get closer, you will see the promise of new life blossoming down here at its base. There *is* life! There is renewal! There is awakening and promise, possibility and hope, when at the center of who and what we are, as individuals and as this church, we seek to understand and possess the Spirit of the Living God falling afresh on us."

This sermon initiated the beginning of a series of services on renewal and positive responses from the congregation. Within a three-month period during and after the series, nine new members, ranging in age from twelve to eighty-two, joined the church. Three of these were baptized. This led to the opportunity to conduct discipleship classes followed by new-member activities and orientation that involved and excited many persons. Usually one or two persons joined the Mayfair Conwell Church at a time, but here were nine new people, a significant (near 10 percent) increase for the congregation. These persons were also the kind who would become involved. Two nights of orientation were held with other church members. They reviewed their history, asked about persons' gifts, and shared about member responsibilities. This was an intentional time of assimilation. According to Marcia, "It felt like God had started the ball rolling!"

From the leadership retreat, the second part of the plan of renewal, came a children's choir. Several persons discovered that individually each had been thinking and praying about such a choir but thought they were alone in their desire. Together they gathered a group of ten to twelve children into a weekly choir which, to the delight of young and old alike, sang regularly in worship. It was a joy for the older members to see the activity and excitement of the children—and fulfilling for the young adult musicians who provided leadership to see their gifts put to good use. It was also wonderful for the children to feel included and important and at the same time learn and have so much fun!

Later that same year, twenty-five adults ranging in ages from twenty-three to eighty spent a unique and valuable weekend on the spiritual life retreat, as projected in the plan of renewal. Old friends were delighted to learn things about each other that they had never imagined before, and new, young couples found important support and friendship with older members. Participants discovered new insights into themselves, others, and God through conversation, activity, meditation, prayer, and play. The closing worship was rich with shared affirmations, empowerment, laughter, tears, joy, and hope! Each participant reported being challenged and enriched like never before. In the closing Sunday morning worship, persons shared how they had seen God in each person. This time of sharing went on and on. A lot of tears were shed as persons affirmed one another. The intimacy and trust built in just two-and-a-half days invigorated the group and spilled over in enthusiasm to the entire congregation. The result was a depth of faith and commitment to each other and to God that the pastor had not seen in these persons before.

A significant postscript speaks to one of the most troubling issues that churches face. In the midst of this renewal, conflict arose within an extended family unit who became disenchanted with the pastor and people alike. While the pastor and church leaders attempted to bring about reconciliation and resolution, most of the congregation were unaware of the struggle. The more the renewal progressed, the more the conflict grew with this small group. The ability of the leadership to take a firm position, confront the conflict, and take appropriate steps was directly linked to the renewed power of God each one experienced and the recommitment to relationship each one had made within. Renewal helped them be with one another during difficult times, and the affirmations of God at work in them solidified their faith and helped at the crucial moments of duress.

"In all," the pastor relates, "I believe that it was God's spirit renewing that has brought about increased energy levels, deeper commitments, and a greater sense of mission and purpose to this congregation. Integration of new members happens with more intentionality and interest. There is greater affirmation for self and others, for who we are and what we are yet to be. There is an excitement—not to increase the numbers for numbers' sake but to invite others to discover what we have found for ourselves—a rich, warm, empowering faith that heals the brokenness and moves us to new heights."

Calvary Baptist

For the Calvary Baptist Church, the plan of renewal was to get the leadership excited about positive things concerning the congregation. Rev. Tommy Jackson felt that the leaders' involvement was necessary to maintain the congregation, to "grow" the congregation, and to do the will of Christ. Using Scriptures like John 13:34-35 on loving one another and Matthew 28:18-20 on making disciples, Rev. Jackson felt that this growth required a reaching in prior to reaching out. Compassion and evangelism were important attitudes for leaders. However, he felt that this would require him to make a change in leadership style, as it was detrimental for the congregation for him to do all of the leadership all of the time.

For a biblical model Rev. Jackson chose Exodus 18. In this portion of Scripture, Moses receives counsel from his father-in-law, Jethro, who admonishes Moses to give up some of his tasks. Delegate and assign responsibility to the tribal leaders. Do not try to do everything, and certainly do not try to do anything alone. Rev. Jackson personally followed Paul's admonition to Timothy to give himself to the Word and to prayer, as he felt a personal need for more time in devotion and commitment. His prayer life was adequate, devotional time was ample, and Bible study was daily, but more was needed; whatever spirituality existed in his life needed strengthening.

In order to implement a new leadership style and to call on the congregation to handle its ministry, Rev. Jackson developed a shepherding plan. Calvary's membership is divided into geographical areas, with a number of deacons assigned to each zone. Visitation had been done by the deacon groups, while the pastor did general visitation. The critical difference with a new shepherding plan was that the pastor and deacons would focus on members with particular spiritual and/or physical needs, which would then be reported to the general congregation. To begin, the deacons would appoint a deacon to be a record keeper for their zone who would coordinate with everyone about the zone members. Each member would have either a quarterly visit or contact from the deacon responsible for their zone.

During these contacts, deacons would encourage faithfulness in family and personal devotions, regular attendance in worship, and sharing in church-related activities. If members needed transportation, the deacon would contact the responsible trustee to arrange for it. The deacon in charge of the zone would take note of people absent from weekly services and would personally deliver or mail a church bulletin. The deacon would report to the deacons' recording secretary the names of any members unable to attend worship. Also, the deacon would notify the secretary of any people who required immediate follow-up due to serious illness, discouragement, interest in Bible studies, or any other needs. Deacons would maintain discretion by bringing confidential reports to the pastor or chair of the deacons.

In a general list of instructions, deacons also had new directions for handling other situations as they would arise. If there was a change of address or other status of members in the zone, the deacon would notify the church secretary. Special items of interest, such as birthdays, anniversaries, promotions, marriages, and graduations would be communicated. If a difficulty existed, the need would be identified before a problem was allowed to fester or grow into a bad situation. Deacons would remain alert for prospective members and for witness opportunities in their zones. Deacons would follow up with visitors who did not have a church home and would visit and invite those persons to share in the ongoing worship at Calvary.

Some other significant activities were projected. When a new person was to be received in Christ, an orientation session would be held by assigned deacons to offer encouragement and give an overview of the church and its doctrines. When there was a death in the congregation, the zone's record keeper would communicate this to the church office, the pastor, and other deacons. As soon as possible the zone deacons and pastor would visit the bereaved family to ascertain needs, assist in making funeral arrangements, and offer words and meals that would encourage those in sorrow.

The deacons would also help in the oversight of the church mission fund. When a need became known, the deacon would work with the deacon chair to respond in consultation with the pastor. Benevolence actions would take place using the deacon body as a whole. The deacons would follow the shepherding plan and improve it as needs arose and response was made.

In order to implement the plan, five training sessions were projected for the deacons. During the sessions the deacons would each receive a copy of the shepherding plan outlining their responsibilities and explore how they could fulfill their roles. In hindsight, Pastor Jackson notes that it would have been better to have implemented the plan in stages with training for the deacons and to have greater congregational involvement in executing the plan. Nevertheless, so far the shepherding plan has resulted in a greater sense of spirituality among the diaconate, and further implementation holds promise of enhanced ministry.

The outcomes to date are exciting. Members, many of whom did not know they had a zone deacon, began to be contacted every three months by their deacon. A ministry of evangelism and caring developed. Most people were very responsive; some who had been out of the church for two or three weeks and received a call from the deacon said they would come back. The deacon's witness made them feel a part of the church, as they knew that there were people beyond the pastor who cared about them. As new members entered the church, a follow-up visit was made by the zone deacon to invite them to attend Sunday school or a discipleship class. After three months these persons were contacted on the regular calling plan. People began to get more involved in the ministry of the church. As a result, people are staying in the church. The congregation is becoming more stable, and people don't get lost but instead are able to get to know one another. They have become a more welcoming congregation, thus realizing one of their goals and dreams.

The new-member class was also implemented. On Wednesday evening an orientation is held before regular prayer meeting. At this time, new people receive an introduction to Calvary Baptist Church. A follow-up discipleship class is held on three Sunday mornings, for a total of four-and-a-half hours of study of the biblical base for the church's beliefs and what it means to be a member of the church. The discovery is that many of the older people are attending along with the newer ones. The excitement is increased as both old and new members join in this endeavor.

Another outgrowth is a new Bible study group. Traditionally two structured groups were held on Wednesdays. The midday group did Bible study, while the evening group offered the opportunity to praise and testify. A new, unstructured group emerged during renewal where people could come with questions. Out of the church renewal focus came the perspective that we should know why we do what we do. Each week, different persons bring questions for exploration.

Response has also grown to members in need. One man who had just entered the church eighteen months before was helping in a men's day program. After a fire broke out in his home, he called a deacon, who asked what kind of help he needed. The member, who did not realize that a benevolence fund existed for this purpose, received the help he needed. In an even more severe situation, the church reached out to a family following a tragic fire near the church in which children were victims of the blaze. Follow-up was done not only with the services but with the family, who was in critical need. Afterward, a broader follow-up was done for people in need in the surrounding community: a shelter program for the homeless was developed, a feeding program was reinstituted, and a clothes closet established. In addition, a food co-op was started to help persons in the church as well as neighbors.

Results are also noted in attendance. Since beginning the process of church renewal and subsequently implementing the shepherding plan, there has been a 35 to 37 percent increase in the church's attendance and response. Earlier 250 bulletins were run for Sunday services; now 400 are needed. Persons are more involved and wanting to do more. Rev. Jackson notes that church renewal has helped him fully understand pastoral delegation, which entails having lay leaders responsible but also helping them know how to do their ministry. On a personal level, he has learned how to take what he calls "the lower road." People become involved, and this gives them a sense of ownership. The renewal plan is working.

Upland Baptist Church

The Upland Baptist Church, under the leadership of Pastor Dale Miller, began to feel the biblical call of Genesis 12:1-3: "Now the LORD said to Abram, 'Go from your country and your kindred and your father's house to the land that I will show you. And I will make of you a great nation, and I will bless you, and make your name great, so that you will be a blessing. I will bless those who bless you, and him who curses you I will curse; and by you all the families of the earth shall bless themselves.' " Using the themes of covenant and blessing, and stressing that spiritual gifts should never be used just for one's own purposes but also for others, Dale projected a plan of renewal by drawing on the strengths of the church, which has a highly committed core of people with a sense of mission to the surrounding community.

The plan of renewal was built in a three-phase process. The first phase was for the pastor to build ownership, receive input, and enlist foundational prayer support through the existing church structure, both with the deacons and in the Wednesday prayer group. The second phase was to draw a "covenanting group" together from the most highly committed members and those with a desire to deepen their faith. This group would go through a process of spiritual gift discernment, mutual support, and plan for mission. Finally, using leadership from this covenanting group, Rev. Miller projected the development of a small group ministry. A variety of "core groups" would be developed to seek to address spiritual needs of the membership as well as to help with the assimilation of new visitors and those on the periphery of the church. The purpose was to help the entire church grow deeper in fellowship and mission through discipleship, Bible study, prayer, and service.

Phase one of this plan has been implemented. Shortly after their annual January meeting, Pastor Dale introduced the plan to the deacons and deaconesses, a group of about eighteen men and women, old and new, who make up the spiritual core of the church's ministry. As they began their planning for the new year, the pastor challenged them with the need for renewal, gave the outline of the plan, and interpreted what it would mean to them as those formally charged with the spiritual care of the congregation. The plan was received warmly. They agreed to be in prayer with the pastor regarding this new direction and began to wrestle with how they could be part of the process.

As they brainstormed together, a new element was added to the renewal plan by the deacons. Each deacon or deaconess already had a congregational list. In an effort to rally the church together and to increase fellowship between members, the deacons decided to plan "cluster gatherings" with members. Four or five clusters would gather for dinner, after which people would share their faith pilgrimages and what brought them into the fellowship of the church. Opportunity would be given to express dreams as well as questions for the deacons or the church at large. These deacon clusters were announced to the church in May, letters sent to each member in July, phone reminders made by deacons and deaconesses in early September, and the gatherings held over five Sundays from mid-September through October. The deacons now had ownership of the plan and a framework was in place for them to participate as well as share the plan for the larger congregation.

In the meantime, starting in February, a second part of phase one unfolded. The pastor began to share some of his dreams for a renewed church with the Wednesday evening prayer and study group. This is a group of about thirty to forty people who make up the informal spiritual core of the congregation. These are people highly committed to prayer, intercession, and the study of God's Word. Through their prayer time and course of study, they had been discussing issues of renewal and service. Now they began to pray intentionally for renewal.

In May another component of the plan was held. To begin the process of having a variety of core groups, the pastor conducted a "spiritual gifts seminar" on a Saturday morning to help educate the congregation concerning spiritual gifts and their biblical basis and to conduct a spiritual gifts index to help discern particular gifts given to individuals for service to the church. Twenty-seven people attended this enlightening time of spiritual growth. They followed the resource *Discover Your Gifts,* [12] which has six study modules that provide a resource to understand gifts, look at biblical foundations, discover one's gifts, confirm such gifts, explore unused gifts, and find out how to use one's gifts. [13] The Saturday morning event began the process of broadening the congregation's understanding of spiritual gifts and how to use them more fully.

By the fall, the outgrowths of phase one were already being felt. For years the pastor had been attempting to encourage the deacons and deaconesses to take on a larger role and to be in more personal contact with the congregation. Now they had set up cluster meetings for the entire congregation. Momentum grew each Sunday night as reports circulated amidst the congregation about the fellowship, faith sharing, and dreaming that began to take place. Approximately 170 people attended the five Sunday evening dinner meetings. There was a lot of fellowship, reviewing and sharing of faith stories, building of relationships between deacons and those on their care lists, and a chance to share dreams and visions for ministry.

Although not planned as a primary part of the deacon clusters, the most significant aspect of the meetings turned out to be hearing persons tell their faith stories. It was exciting to hear what had brought people to faith in Christ and the church and to learn of significant people and events along their journeys of faith. The pastor had the "Baptismal Record Book" on hand, which listed names back to 1852 and gave them a sense of history, belonging, and growth. The people saw themselves afresh as God's people—who they had been, who they are, and, with God's help, who they can be.

As much as these deacon's clusters have had an effect on the congregation at large, the most meaningful growth has been realized in a renewed understanding of what it means for the deacons and deaconesses to be spiritual leaders in the midst of the congregation. They now have a greater understanding of those who have been given to their care. But most of all the pastor reports that "we have a greater understanding as pastor and leaders what it means to be in ministry together as we deeply depend on each other for the spiritual care and growth of the church."

The second phase of the plan for renewal is a follow-up to the spiritual gifts seminar and the covenanting group. In the fall, the church conducted a six-month follow-up to its spiritual gifts seminar. It was exciting for the group to be together again, and, after taking the spiritual gifts index and meeting with the pastor independently, two more persons were added to the original group. New energy was felt as they reviewed some of the biblical materials on gifts and joined in prayer that included requests for discernment of given and dreams for the larger church community.

In the follow-up workshop, the leadership encouraged those who had begun to identify and implement their gifts in ministry and supported those who were still going through the spiritual search. There were moments of celebration over what God had accomplished through them and amazement that so much had taken place in ministry. Even those still searching for God's leading sensed a peace and an inner confidence that God had gifted them and would provide, in God's time, the opportunity to serve.

The group members began to strategize how they might continue to encourage one another and hold one another accountable for the use of what God had entrusted to them and the church for ministry. It was decided that starting in January they would meet for dinner for prayer, study, and encouragement one Wednesday evening a month before the normal Bible study and prayer time. Starting with the nucleus of twenty, they would keep opening the group to include others who wanted to go deeper in their faith journey. The ideas continued to flow and anticipation to build for what this covenant group could mean to the participants and the larger church family. Part of the projection for the upcoming January through May was the formation of small group ministries or "core groups."

The process so far has not been without pain. Stress has come at different times from different directions. The pastor reflects, "It has been difficult to introduce a new plan in a church that already has a very busy calendar for ministry. It has been a struggle to release some people from old responsibilities with the idea of doing something new. It has been hard to set priorities and plan a way that the most significant ministries for renewal can occur. It is at times stressful to change from just being busy as a church to becoming renewed by the Spirit and alive in mission. A secondary stress has come as we have learned to depend on one another in new ways. The old expectations and roles, particularly of our deacons and deaconesses, are changing. We are learning to support one another in these changing roles."

In the midst of the plan, there has been significant growth in relationships and shared goals for ministry. A sense of renewal has taken place. On the congregational level, there is a renewed sense of belonging to a growing fellowship with a vital mission. Slowly a new sense of that mission is emerging from within the core of the congregation. The deacons have planned programs and have been in conversation with those in their care. Most of all, the pastor reports, "We have a greater understanding as pastor and leaders of what it means to be in ministry together as we deeply depend on each other for the spiritual care and growth of the church." As the plan continues to emerge, the pastor reports that the enthusiasm continues to build in worship, study groups, and servant ministries.

As the deacon groups were concluding and the second part of the gifts seminar was held, the church celebrated a meaningful day of welcoming eight new members to the church as they affirmed faith in Jesus Christ in a service of baptism. The stage had been set during the deacon cluster meetings for a real time of spiritual celebration. New people are being warmly received and incorporated into the life of the church. It is exciting to see new relationships build and new people entering actively into ministry. Six of the eight who joined the church shared that they were excited about their plans to go to a local mission in the city of Chester to provide a meal during the Christmas holidays. They had a clear sense of joy about being a part of the church and about doing something meaningful for Christ and for others.

The discovery for this congregation is that it is in renewing the covenantal relationship with the Lord that we are blessed, renewed, and become spiritually alive. In this context, God's people learn what it means to be a people of blessing—receiving blessing and being vehicles of blessing. However, they felt that renewing covenant must never be for our own privilege or selfish spiritual gain but rather for God's purposes. The church is called for mission. According to the apostle Paul, the Spirit gives gifts to be used in service, uplifting and building up the church (1 Corinthians 12:4-7). As Pastor Dale reports, "I'm learning through this process that renewal happens in ebbs and flows." As ministries are prayed for, planned, and experienced, a tremendous amount of spiritual energy is generated. A healthy exhaustion is part of the process, for as they have spent ourselves, renewal occurs as God restores them again to worship and to serve.

Chapter 8

The Path to Joy

A new heart and a new spirit permeate a congregation's life when it is undergoing renewal. New life is evident as people begin to have new priorities, new commitments, new enthusiasm. What happens for individuals happens for congregations, too. The structures change; new dynamics are at work. People reach out in mission and service. A renewing church is one in which certain dynamics of transformation can be identified: a personal faith, an openness in style, a confidence and motivation of members. A church undergoing renewal becomes a nurturing body, a worshiping congregation, and a witnessing and serving church. A new heart and a new spirit are in formation, new dynamics develop, and new life breaks forth!

A Personal Pilgrimage of Faith

In renewal, members embark on a personal pilgrimage of faith. As they discover their ministry and become engaged in service, they begin to learn of the reality of God by reflecting on God's leading and by sharing about God's presence during routine tasks. Laborers can discover that God is with them on this deeper journey because persons growing in their ministries are growing in their faith. As one woman so aptly said, "I'm growing, and therefore *we're* growing."

As persons feel like they're reaching their limits in service, they can learn to depend on God more fully. Questions will arise, especially when some task seems hopeless or when attempts to help do not succeed. Properly handled, such questions can point people to exploring their faith. Individuals can discover the grace of God, the reality of God, and the unfolding mystery of God. In renewal, persons delve into the whole faith journey told in the Scriptures. They can identify with prophets like Ezekiel, who envisioned a new heart and a new spirit; with the apostle Paul, who saw God's grace reaching out to all people; with John on the Isle of Patmos, who spoke God's message to churches facing hardship.

In renewal we live in the biblical story and message.

Individuals with a hunger for renewal need guidance about their own personal devotional lives. A plan of renewal for a church could well include a unit for all members focused on enhancing their devotional lives. Such a unit could develop resources and mutual support. Some excellent videos are available that feature a potter, an insurance executive, a foreman, and a judge whose discovery of their ministry led to deep inner renewal that overflowed to the lives of other persons.[1]

An elective class could be taught in the adult, youth, and children's education departments. A life of prayer could be the topic for small groups; resources could be studied and prayer disciplines established.[2] In one of the renewal projects recorded in this book, the traditional Wednesday evening Bible study and prayer group became an integral part in the renewal of the congregation. Entire denominations can engage in such an endeavor. In one denomination leaders have called on the entire denomination to be in prayer for renewal early Monday morning, while in another denomination there is a regional and national focus on renewal.[3] Prayerfulness alerts us to the deep inner movings of God in renewal personally, as congregations, and as denominations.

The transformation that begins within persons in ministry spills over into all that happens in the church. The title of the Sunday school project looking at other Sunday schools that were growing was changed from "The Successful Sunday School" to "The Transformational Sunday School"[4]—because people's lives were being changed. A district representative from one of the denominations who was present for an on-site meeting spoke about the way adults have their lives changed by discovering the gospel in daily life. The contagious quality of being transformed could be felt over and over upon entering the churches being studied. Persons would tend to the needs of this visitor and also share about the life of their church. An invitation was also extended: "Why don't you come back to worship with us?" As pastors in the church renewal course have indicated, the felt need for renewal began within them and spread to key leaders and then to others in the church. Churches with a new heart and a new spirit become inviting and open congregations.

Openness as a Congregation

Besides helping persons discover a first-person faith, a renewing church is one developing an openness in many aspects of its life. As already noted in this resource, there are many types of congregations varying in location, composition, and background. All have certain characteristics, however, such as ground rules and understandings among members, many of which are unwritten. These characteristics suggest a continuum from a closed to an open congregation.

A closed congregation operates strongly on precedent. Lethargy builds because decisions are almost automatic and persons fear to risk even exploring alternatives to the present life. More than traditionalism is at work in such a church. Looking a bit deeper, we see decisions are not made in the committee or board meetings. Rather, persons make decisions informally in the parking lot or over the telephone. This informal method of decision making is supported by the informal method of communication. "Did you hear?" is the way to share what is happening. Persons hold the same job for many years, even when a sense of purpose is absent. The closed congregation often speaks of evangelism as a need or a must but has not found ways to help new members become assimilated and become part of the congregational decision-making process. The vibrancy of faith is lost when all that is done becomes routine.

Renewal transforms a closed congregation into an open congregation. Miracles of faith and ownership happen in the renewing church. Such a congregation has found renewal not as a wishful dream but as a journey of finding a significant lifestyle and ministry.[5] Communication becomes more open and formal, with written memos and agendas of meetings mailed or posted. Good decisions are made at meetings where the Holy Spirit is leading, and follow-up and accountability are built in so that decisions are implemented. Outcomes are affirmed and celebrated. Offices become more intentional positions of service; job descriptions become more clearly delineated. The emphasis is on meeting the needs of people both inside and outside the congregation. The congregation begins to have new life.

Entry into the open congregation becomes easier because commonly owned goals define an intentional group to which persons can belong. Acceptance is no longer gauged by knowing people for a stated number of years or by coming from a certain family. Nor are persons ostracized because of their background or because they are from a certain family. Diversity is no longer seen as a threat but as a strength of the group to fulfill varied needs. The open congregation uses people's gifts and potential, and individuals feel affirmed. The invitation to join in is extended in a very powerful way.

The open congregation begins to discover dynamics that go beyond accepting others. The future opens up because this church is not just responding to crises; it is planning its life according to its vision and is open to what God is doing. Decisions are solid decisions because there is follow-up. This congregation begins to discover larger challenges than it ever dreamed possible. It discovers that its life is its own; its walls are its own; its worship is its own. The open congregation may find it can dispose of or use the many odds and ends that accumulate around a church's building without fear of hurting someone's feelings. This congregation has a high life expectancy.[6]

Most congregations are actually a combination of these two styles. Each congregation is on a continuum that is not linear but is multifaceted, with many factors working to draw it either to decline or to life. What a church does with tradition, pressures, precedents, and the needs of its people has a lot to say about its vitality. The processes can be seen in the movements of renewal suggested in Psalm 51. As we turn upward and then inward, a new heart is discovered in the secret recesses of the human being in touch with God. As openness develops, a new spirit is demonstrated in the deep abiding union with God, which results in action in the church's life.

Confidence and Motivation

A healthy self-confidence and a good self-image are as important for a church as they are for an individual. When a church is not in renewal, forces are often at work behind the scenes, controlling the church's life without anyone being aware of them; these so-called hidden agendas express the unresolved issues of people within the congregation. Unnamed, such factors can impede renewal. A transformation is needed so that persons can gain confidence as a church, relate openly to one another, and have a clear sense of purpose.

Feeding into such a malaise is often a fear of self-expression. Persons feel others will not listen to them or will misconstrue what they say. These fears indicate a lack of trust and lack of focus. This type of church is not owned by its members because they are afraid to express how they think things should happen and therefore have shied away from investing in what does happen. How many church programs fail because people vote with their feet? Loss of self-image and fear of self-expression impede vitality.

Renewal reverses these trends. A congregation begins to feel a sense of healthy pride. Developing a focus gives people a goal; an unfolding plan of renewal gives a sense of satisfaction. An identity begins to form as persons see their strengths used in ministries that are affecting people's lives. People begin to express themselves more comfortably. In the transformational Sunday school project, one church leader felt it was characteristic of his church that new persons were put to work and gained self-confidence by being able to participate. Encouraging such sharing became a hallmark of this church.

Such a transformation is seen in many little things. Persons can become creative if they are not worried that everything must be perfect; participation is a way to express their faith. Classroom teachers can have students make items to take home for their families or have a class share a piece of their work in worship. Art objects can be displayed in the hallways; banners can be hung for specific occasions. A collage of pictures from a retreat can be displayed in the lobby. A center of worship for the senior adults group can be part of Sunday's worship service. Part of a service project from a youth trip could be a focus for worship. A congregation undergoing renewal looks for opportunities to make self-expression part of church life. One of the aspects of a transformed congregation is that persons share gifts. We saw how identification of gifts became part of the renewal plan of one of the congregations. Encouraging such growth is at the heart of this renewal process.

A transforming church also addresses the area of motivation. One of the most difficult questions is what to do when nobody seems to want to do anything. At this point the problems seem larger than the solutions. For my classes in church renewal, participants spend one evening either alone or with a group identifying strengths of their congregation. Class members invariably return to the class sessions with a new perspective. This shift from seeing only deficits to affirming strengths is important in motivation. Persons must catch a glimpse of purpose for being a church.

In affirming a new heart and a new spirit, the psalmist turned upward to God and then inward in reflection. As leadership gains a new sense of God's love and helps persons explore their strengths and their identity as the church, people become more excited about investing in the work of Christ. This search for purpose begins as they are responsive to needs and to the purpose of their existence. Then it becomes more clear what they are striving for as the church. When this becomes clear, they can feel that it is worthwhile to invest their lives, and renewal begins, motivation increases, and purpose is discovered.

Discovering gifts and ministries also addresses the crucial area of active people dropping out of the church. Analysis of lay leader burnout shows that a clear assessment of gifts and calling, along with implementing that calling with a sense of vocation, is critical in offsetting fatigue and disillusionment. The church must begin with its vital resource of people and help them discover their calling. Understanding vocation is integral to energizing persons in ministry.[7] Identification of gifts can be part of this process. Persons must then have definite job descriptions and a clear focus. Follow-up should happen after an assignment to a ministry is made. Crucial to keeping people motivated and properly employed in the church is the renewal process described in this resource—especially assessing needs and matching the strengths of people with those needs so that they can grow in their ministry. The process of enlisting, contracting, and supervising described in the previous chapters are all components of keeping persons motivated.[8]

Most important in all ministry is growing deeper in faith. We need to ask where persons can become involved so that they have the opportunity to express their faith and grow spiritually. Crucial will be the supervision process described in Chapter 5, which stresses the importance of spiritual direction so that persons can make the connection between growing in ministry and growing in their faith. Just as important will be renewing events in the life of the church, into which persons come as coworkers, sometimes energized and sometimes depleted from life's tasks of ministry. A nurturing environment will be important in worship, education, and fellowship activities in which enrichment of faith is key.[9]

A Nurturing Community

Nurture is essential for a church in renewal. In discovering a new heart and a new spirit, people will seek opportunities to grow in their faith. Nurture entails all aspects of training, support, spiritual guidance, and enrichment. In the context of the faith environment, nurture is part of the inner sustaining of the church, both of individuals and of the congregation itself. Persons will find that the atmosphere of the church is a vital component to growing in faith. The nurturing environment encourages growth. Just as a plant grows when it is properly cultivated, watered, and pruned, so both individuals and a congregation become vibrant as all aspects of their development are cared for and nurtured.

One area for nurture long overlooked in the local church has been the Sunday school. The Bush Creek congregation realized that fifty-two existing Sunday school sessions a year could be used to strengthen the faith and lives of people of all ages. Rather than beginning with children's classes, the impetus for nurture began at the adult level. The adult curriculum came to have new significance as we began to ask what persons wanted to learn. Rather than letting a class flounder with this question, a lot of work was done in order to assess the broad range of needs of adults and to find workable resources to teach the class. The needs of participants, as well as the resources available, were the beginning points for developing a well-rounded series of classes.

The need developed for upgrading the skills of teachers in the children's classes as teachers were rotated and teams replaced solo teaching. Teacher-training workshops provided the necessary skills and sharing as well as needed support to risk the adventure of teaching. Soon new persons began to teach. In turn, interest emerged in teacher training in the adult areas, and persons began to teach who never expected that they had the skills. They also began to explore topics they never imagined they would have interest in. Rather than equating learning with obtaining information, they came to see education as an experience in which to engage. The transformation to meaningful Christian education can provide basic nurture of persons in a congregation.

Another possibility for nurture in the local church is through small groups. Small groups usually arise out of special interests or age groups, such as youth, senior adults, or parents without partners. Such groups develop out of felt needs and with a rather specific agenda. Each can provide support, do training, and lead to growth of persons in a faith environment. Sometimes the agenda can help persons wrestle with issues and broaden their perspective. Humor in groups can help overcome the valleys, and, in an atmosphere of trust, persons can develop a sense of being sustained by God.

The ongoing establishment of the church's covenant for renewal sustains a nurturing environment. All leaders as well as staff can continually lift up other individuals in prayer and in support. Nurture begins with the hospitality shown to strangers, continues with the attention to the routine needs of the congregation, and extends to those who have specific needs. In this process we learn that as we serve the "least" among us—those who can be easily overlooked, including the stranger—we discover the Christ in our midst. Giving attention to those in another family, another generation, another situation is the nurturing task. Such attention takes the form not only of formal events but also the general interactions of the congregation in its life as a body.

In working with the handicapped, Jean Vanier of the L'Arche movement has helped us learn more about the nature of Christian community and the dynamics of the nurturing spirit.[10] For Vanier, the source of nourishment is in the hearts of the "little people," in the wounded and the handicapped. Rather than looking at nurture in terms of the so-called healthy group providing something to the weaker group, Vanier lifts up how the disenfranchised often become the bread for others through mutual commitment and mutual concern. By discovering the light of Christ, the presence of Christ in each other, persons become bread one for another.[11] The nurturing task becomes part of the heart of the renewing church as people lift one another up.

In terms of spiritual guidance and ministry, often the deacons and deaconesses of the congregation take on this role to help the pastor, providing specific services like communion or anointing. In meeting with the deacon committee, the renewal committee could explore how nurture can extend to persons providing ministry to one another. Some churches develop a prayer chain or have people praying for specific people each week. Many models can be explored. While the deacons or a nurture committee usually take responsibility for initiating this vital function, everyone can become part of nurturing the faith of others.

Sometimes this nurture comes from the least expected source. In one congregation persons often spoke of the reward of coming to the Sunday service. While the obvious assumption would be that they came because of the service and the preaching, there was actually an additional reason. One person mentioned that the greeting by a particular usher at the front door meant so much in her life of faith, and the regularity of the encouragement at the front door had sustained her over the years. Such nurturing can come from many sources and in many different ways. The renewal committee can explore how the church can intentionally cultivate a nurturing atmosphere, which is essential for growth and vitality.

Enrichment is the final aspect of nurture. Sometimes a ministry might feature a guest speaker, or a special trip might result from a Bible study group, or a ministry is begun that takes people to the subway to hold discussions with young adults waiting there. Missionaries and other guest speakers can help them explore an area of their life. A service worker in the church's outreach ministries can be invited for a dinner. Enrichment opens up a whole arena to help persons grow in faith. The Christian education or nurture board could spend some creative time helping to identify resources to expand the church's horizons. With planning, such enrichment can become an exciting part of church life.

Faith is therefore intentionally developed. The dynamic of nurture can be present in the church when persons are strengthened in their faith, challenged in their development of skills, and given the support to meet their tasks in life and ministry. As we saw in Psalm 51, a key in the transformation of renewal is forgiveness. Often in the work of nurture, forgiveness becomes real. People extend themselves over barriers and situations in order to lift others up. The gospel becomes real and faith comes alive as people are growing in their sense of God's presence and leading. Transformation occurs, and a new heart and a new spirit become reality.

A Worshiping Congregation

Another dynamic of a church undergoing renewal is that members feel a need for corporate experiences of worship. Such experiences help affirm the faith that guides them as a body of believers engaged in ministry. Images of faith can be creatively expressed in order to capture the power of the gospel. Joys can be celebrated; concerns can be lifted up. Persons can be drawn beyond individual struggles to sense a group affirmation of mutual commitments. Set in the context of the faith environment, persons stop to recall their purpose and to affirm the loyalty that keeps them sustained. Worship is their wellspring of support as they discover the drama of God's activity in their lives.

Worship became much more central to the life of the Bush Creek congregation as it underwent renewal. As persons gave of themselves, a greater sense of need for worship developed. In the second year of the plan for ministry, worship was identified as a focal area to aid in the life of the congregation. An emphasis on preaching brought a new intentionality to the worship experience. A preaching unit was done so that the pastor could grow in preaching. An outgrowth of this unit was a "worship arts task group," which began to plan for meaningful worship. Attendance increased significantly as the church came alive in renewal.

Worship emerges both as a need and as a response. Persons begin to discover how vital worship is to their lives. If they are engaged in ministry, they will find that they have expended a lot during the week and need to feel replenished. This is one of the reasons why every worship service should incorporate the sharing of the Good News. The Good News speaks of grace for the human predicament and proclaims the presence of Christ to feed our hunger for spiritual bread. Worship lifts up the vital message that we are God's beloved, that such love is unconditional, and that God restores the soul, heart, and spirit.[12] Worship is also a response to God's reaching out into our lives. We discover the call of God and listen to God's will in our lives. Like Jesus, we draw away in order to come back to further engage. Indeed, persons come to worship to recall their purpose, to affirm God's power and strength, and to discover God's activity in their lives.

If renewal is occurring in a congregation, a fundamental shift occurs in the experience of worship. Servant leaders begin viewing persons as coworkers in ministry who are in need of being replenished with the Good News of God's love. This is a tremendous transformation in approach. The congregation praises God together, asks for God's forgiveness, receives pardon, looks for God's challenge in their lives, and responds to God's calling. (See Isaiah 6:1-8.) This shared nature of worship is a vital component of faith.

Such a transformation will mean an entirely new approach to preaching. Rather than viewing the sermon as what the preacher can get across to the congregation, those in preaching will begin to see where the congregation is at present and to explore how the Good News of the gospel can come alive in their lives—how to speak a word of freedom for their situation. Rather than being a mute proclamation within cloistered walls, the spoken word becomes the sharing of Good News with persons engaged in struggles as equal partners in ministry. Rather than preaching at the congregation, the minister speaks of the light of God's presence from within the context of a common life. The gospel is the freeing component that speaks of freedom, obedience, and joy. In worship we find ourselves within the biblical story with fellow pilgrims who are discovering deliverance.

Several resources are available to help in developing such a style of preaching. Merrill Abbey developed the idea of a work sheet for preaching that begins with people's needs and correlates what word the biblical text would convey to address those needs or situations.[13] Abbey suggests seven steps to such a process: diagnosis, prescription, exposition, experience, program, purpose, and proposition. Under purpose, for example, the preacher must decide if the purpose is to inform, convince, inspire, or move to action. All this leads to writing a single sentence that declares how the gospel can speak to the needs of this day and situation.[14]

In a similar way, James Forbes has worked with the concept of partnering in the delivery of sermons. In this style, the one delivering the message shows respect for the congregation by treating them as partners in the task of communicating the gospel. The preacher first listens to the congregation. When a question is posed, the preacher gives time for the congregation to answer in their own minds. The preacher is curious about what listeners are thinking, how they are responding, and what to do together with the message of the text. Partnering conveys to people that the preacher is with them in exploring the dynamics of the text as it relates to their felt needs at that time.[15]

Being intentional in worship, both in the service and in the preaching, conveys that worship is essential to renewal of the church. By proclaiming the Good News in the midst of the human situation, servant leaders address human needs with the power of the gospel of Jesus Christ. Transformation is possible; new life can spring forth. What has restricted life before no longer holds sway. Hope is real. This basic message needs to be affirmed and proclaimed. Worship can be part of the transformation of a congregation as hope is claimed in the lives of people. God continues to reach out; God never gives up. Grace unbounded always shines forth.

A Witnessing and Serving Church

While the church is nurturing its members and worship is becoming an essential part of the Christian life, it is witness and service that keep a church from becoming ingrown. As long as members concentrate only on their own lives, their perspective is narrow and not totally in accord with the gospel message. Not only will their gifts be limited, but the church's entire life will ultimately suffer. In the transformation of renewal, the church learns that in reaching out the congregation actually grows within. In fact, members return with new perspectives and insights into their own situation. Changes occur as persons sense the needs of others. The transformation in renewal is that persons *want* to reach out.

Service can take on many forms, from witnessing in word to serving in the name of Christ for a special project or cause. Such witness and service is not done to soothe one's own conscience or to fulfill all the needs in the world but to express compassion from the heart as a faith response. Witness is a response to the Great Commission; service is a response to the parable of the good Samaritan. As Martin Luther so aptly said, Jesus was the man for others. In the words he spoke as well as in the countless deeds of kindness he did, Jesus reached out to others. The dynamic of service is crucial in the renewal process because it speaks of living out the gospel.

The witness of the Bush Creek congregation increased significantly during its renewal process. One major emphasis was on collecting money for the hungry by members placing small cups on their dinner tables. In another project, some of the women used old bandage-rolling machines to roll pieces of sheets for casts for disaster relief areas. Witness within the congregation became a new emphasis. Furthermore, witness called for reaching out to new families by visiting them, sending them newsletters, and inviting them to small groups or other functions of the church. By widening the circles of care, everyone was enriched. The church discovered that discipleship calls for response to needs both large and small.

A church with a growing sense of witness and service discovers the needs within its walls, in the community, and in the wider world. Giving out Bibles, taking clothing to those in need, and relating to new persons in the community are all within the scope of meeting needs. Being a witness will stretch one's own resources while also influencing the character of the church. A church learns to lose its life in order to find it. New resources are discovered within as a church reaches out. Witness provides a thrust for discipleship that never allows us to give up. The character of a church is fundamentally changed by reaching out.

If nurture develops our faith and worship develops our hope, then certainly witness completes the New Testament trilogy with love (1 Corinthians 13:13). Witness proclaims charity or love. The love of God is expressed in word and deed in the church that is being renewed. Such love is transformational; its power is felt and experienced. If one thing speaks to individuals, it is love become real. Witness and service keeps a church from becoming ingrown. Church members begin to learn about one another, about their neighbors, and about their world. Often a real witness grows out of helping others, and compassion expands the hearts of those reaching out. Whereas before a church may have felt it did not have enough resources and was focused on keeping what it had, now the church begins to see how love can reach out, and in so doing it discovers new life. A new heart and a new spirit has to do not only with reaching in but also with reaching out. We learn this in a unique way by returning to Psalm 51.

Joy

"Fill me with joy and gladness" is the prayer of the psalmist. In renewal this prayer is realized. Herein is the third movement of renewal: the movement outward. Grace becomes real, and new life is discovered. The psalmist is delivered from despair. Transformation happens within, resulting in joy. When a genuine renewal comes within, it moves a person toward service. Rather than offering outer sacrifices, the psalmist sees renewal turning one's very being over to God. "The sacrifice acceptable to God is a broken spirit; a broken and contrite heart, O God, thou wilt not despise" (Psalm 51:17). This new nature is according to God's spirit. The psalmist is able to express poetically the experience of such new life. "Restore to me the joy of thy salvation . . ." (v. 12). God's action within is felt and realized, and the outcome is praise, thanksgiving, and joy.

Joy has deep meaning in renewal. Joy is growing in our understanding of God. In each church featured in this book, members had their understanding of God expanded and grew closer to God as they saw how they and others experienced heartfelt change. Joy is sharing in that reconciling power of God's love. The Anchor Bible translates verse 14 as: "Give me again your saving joy and by your generous spirit sustain me."[16] In renewal, the saving power of God becomes real, and God's generous nature becomes clear. The natural response is joy, for one is uplifted. Joy has the nature of surprise, as God's love breaks in on us with grace unbounded. Joy is the serendipity of the unexpected; the spontaneous result of joy is to reach outward.

In the three movements of renewal, joy follows the reach upward and inward by reaching outward. We see this clearly in the New Testament. In the raising of Lazarus, we see the spontaneous nature of joy as God's work was realized. This same joy is evident in the resurrection stories (such as Luke 24:41). The unique aspect of joy is that it is often discovered while undergoing hardship. In fact, God's power to transform is experienced when in our weakness God's love brings forth new life.[17] We feel a unique joy, for God is victorious. In response we feel a need to reach out.

Reaching out across the barriers that could otherwise hinder new life is shown in dramatic ways in the renewing church. In 2 Corinthians, the apostle Paul is in the midst of his own church renewal project. Part of the question includes the poverty of the Jerusalem church as well as the struggles in the church at Corinth, where factions and strife lead to a unique challenge. Behind Paul is the early council of the church at Jerusalem, which has discerned how Christians of Jewish descent and Christians of Gentile descent were to deal with what it meant to be in Christ and to support one another (Acts 15).

In that context Paul takes up a collection of the churches from the Gentile Christians. In Macedonia Christians were undergoing their own kind of hardship. These Gentile Christians, however, took up a collection for the Jewish Christians back in the home church in Jerusalem. This provided a real witness to the church of Corinth, "for in a severe test of affliction, their abundance of joy and their extreme poverty have over-flowed in a wealth of liberality on their part" (2 Corinthians 8:2). Real healing occurs as people reach out across barriers because of God's redeeming action experienced in their hearts. The root cause of their joy is clear: "First they gave themselves to the Lord and to us by the will of God" (2 Corinthians 8:5). They discover the dynamic relationship with God in Christ by giving out of their joy. A new heart and a new spirit create a joy that propels us to charity towards others.

Understanding the nature of God's redeeming action causes us to reach outward. Each of the churches in this book discovered how inextricably renewal was bound to service to others. In matching strengths with needs, this dynamic of renewal was established. We saw that in our triangle of spiritual growth (Chapter 2) as new life would come forth. In teaching church renewal, I have been profoundly touched by the many stories of congregations who reached out to persons within as well as to those in their communities and in the world at large. Every church and every church study points to service as being key in the renewal effort. Joy causes people to reach out. Further study of 2 Corinthians reveals how the benevolences given are called charity or love. Joy happens in giving relief, the word that technically means "ministry."[18] Out of response to God's love, those who engage in the ministry of service experience joy. That is the nature of transformation of the gospel.

Joy was clear in the face of the women who told of the exact number of nails driven by church members who put on a new roof themselves so that the money saved could help feed the hungry. Joy was in the eyes of those who described their transformational Sunday school and their outreach ministry with the handicapped. Joy was in the eyes of teachers who described how their rural children invited inner-city youth to their facility and also went to the inner-city church for Christian fellowship. Joy was in the eyes of those reaching out in ministry to street people who discovered the gospel and became part of a growing, dynamic city church. Joy is in a children's ministry reaching out to Native American youth and discovering self-worth and dignity. Joy is hearing how a country parish began to reach out to others in ministry and found a whole new life. Joy is the gospel realized, as people are transformed by God's love in Christ and then reach out across all boundaries to share the gospel with others.

Joy has the nature of the unexpected. What was wanted in the church happens, but often in a different way than anticipated. Sometimes persons look for the old glory to return, but the new life comes in entirely unexpected ways. We look in one direction for new life, but growth occurs in a different direction than previously known. Rather than something that is that far removed or brought in by someone, new life emerges from within. New life comes in the most unexpected ways. As with the story of the raising of Lazarus, God acts as life-giver.[19] Glory can return to our lives as old structures are transformed to new life. The grave cloths are removed, and the church become responsive, open, free. New energy and joy breaks forth.

Often such joy is realized through struggle. It is not without pain, for that is the nature of growth. What we have explored in this handbook is a process of responding to the promises of the gospel. Nothing is ever perfect, but we are on the way in our journey. The gospel's power is breaking in on our lives, and humbly we receive the new life. We feel God stirring within. As with Lazarus, we must unbind and let go. The journey of renewal is just that. Using our human efforts, God transforms imperfect creatures into a people of God. A new heart and a new spirit are the gifts of renewal. Such new life spells joy!

As the church reaches out in renewal, God enables us and so draws us to his living presence, as Jude (vv. 24-25) proclaimed using a moving doxology of joy:[20]

Now to him who is able to keep you from falling and to present you without blemish before the presence of his glory with rejoicing, to the only God, our Savior through Jesus Christ our Lord, be glory, majesty, dominion, and authority, before all time and now and for ever. Amen.

NOTES

Chapter 1

1. Roy M. Oswald and Speed B. Leas, *The Inviting Church* (Washington, D.C.: The Alban Institute, 1987), 69ff.

Chapter 2

1. Richard Germann and Peter Arnold, *Job and Career Building* (New York: Harper and Row, 1980), 38.

2. Richard Bolles, *What Color Is Your Parachute?* (Berkeley: Ten Speed Press, 1972). This excellent resource in vocational direction is revised on a yearly basis.

3. David S. Young, "Sunday Schools that Transform," *Builder* (February 1989), 19.

4. Such factors were among those identified in the successful Sunday schools. See Young, "Sunday Schools," 11-19.

5. Roy M. Oswald and Speed B. Leas, *The Inviting Church* (Washington, D.C.: The Alban Institute, 1987), 18.

6. Ibid., 19.

7. Arlin Rothauge, *Sizing Up a Congregation for New Member Ministry* (New York: The Episcopal Church Center, n.d.). Order from the Episcopal Church Center, 815 Second Ave., New York, NY 10017. Also see the follow-up resource, *Reshaping a Congregation for a New Future.*

8. Such concepts as focusing and rightsizing instead of diversifying and expanding have been developed by a team in leadership at Pennsylvania State University, after struggling with the complexity of need in higher education while also being called more and more to solve the world's problems. See "Observations from the President" by Joab Thomas in *Report to Parents and Families,* Pennsylvania State University, Spring 1993, 1-2.

9. J. W. Lawrie, "Leadership and Magical Thinking," *Personnel Journal,* September 1970, 750-56.

10. David S. Young, "How the Pastor Can Help Motivate and Supervise Renewal in the Local Congregation," D.Min. Thesis, Bethany Theological Seminary, 1976, 24-25.

11. Robert Greenleaf, *The Servant as Leader* (Cambridge: Center for Applied Studies, 1973), citing Hermann Hesse, *The Journey to the East* (New York: The Noonday Press, 1956), 1, 2.

12. Ibid., 1.

13. Ibid., 2.

14. Hermann Beyer, "Diakonia," in Gerhard Kittel, ed., *Theological Dictionary of the New Testament,* trans. and ed. Geoffrey W. Bromiley, D.Litt., D.D. (Grand Rapids: Wm. B. Eerdmans Publishing Co., 1964-1972), 2:87.

15. An outstanding work on Christ the servant is T. W. Manson, *Ministry and Priesthood: Christ's and Ours* (Richmond: John Knox Press, n.d.), 26-31.

16. The Robert Greenleaf Center for Servant Leadership (1100 W. 42d St., Suite 321, Indianapolis, IN 46208) is an excellent resource center for broad application of the servant-leadership concept.

17. Greenleaf, *The Servant as Leader,* 10.

18. Ibid., 16.

19. Ibid., 23.

20. Ibid., 23-25.

21. Ibid., 7.

22. Ibid., 22.

23. Young, "Sunday Schools," 19.

Chapter 3

1. Robert Greenleaf, *The Servant as Leader* (Cambridge: Center for Applied Studies, 1973), 32.

2. For more on the role of the anticipatory style of leadership, see Lyle Schaller, *The Change Agent: The Strategy of Innovative Leadership* (Nashville: Abingdon Press, 1972).

3. Logos System Associates, 1405 Frey Rd,, Philadelphia, PA 15235.

4. See Robert Mager, *Preparing Instructional Objectives* (Belmont: Lear Siegler, Inc., 1962), for a description of writing objectives.

5. David S. Young, "Marks of Ministry," *Messenger,* May 1976, 14-15. Elaborates five marks of ministry from the Gospel of John that were the basis of the doctoral project, "How the Pastor Can Help Motivate and Supervise Renewal in the Local Congregation."

Chapter 4

1. Logos System Associates, 1405 Frey Road, Philadelphia, PA 15235.

2. James Moss, *People Spots* (Harrisburg, Pa.: Churches of God, General Conference, 1988), 76-86.

3. An excellent resource on spiritual gifts is *Discover Your Gifts* (Grand Rapids: Church Development Resources, 1983).

Chapter 5

1. In its original form, this chapter by the author is included in an anthology

on lay ministry. Reprinted from *Calling of the Laity* by Verna Dozier with permission from the Alban Institute, Inc. 4125 Nebraska Ave., NW, Washington, D.C. 20016. Copyright 1988. All rights reserved.

2. Parish Consultation Skills Training, Mid-Atlantic District Church of the Brethren, New Windsor, Md,, January 26-28, 1972.

3. Resources on age groups can be located by writing to one's curriculum office. Often a teacher's guide or other resource is available that describes characteristics of the age one is teaching. The Provident Book Finder is another excellent resource; contact the Mennonite Publishing House, 616 Walnut Ave., Scottdale, PA 15683-1999.

4. Consult your denominational offices for available film resources.

5. For the connection of servant leadership and in-depth prayer, I am indebted to Henri Nouwen and his written correspondence to me on servanthood and deep prayer of October 29, 1986. The outcomes are noted in supervision of others in ministry.

6. See resources by Douglas Steere, *Dimensions of Prayer* (New York: Women's Division, General Board of Global Ministries of the United Methodist Church, 1962) and *Gleanings* (Nashville: The Upper Room, 1986). Also see Thomas Kelly, *A Testament of Devotion* (New York: Harper and Row, 1941) and Richard Foster, *Prayer: Finding the Heart's New Home* (San Francisco: Harper, 1992).

7. Roy M. Oswald with Jackie McMakin, *How to Prevent Lay Leader Burnout* (Washington, D.C.: The Alban Institute, Inc., 1984).

8. Douglas Johnson, *The Care and Feeding of Volunteers* (Nashville: Abingdon, 1978).

9. Oswald, 5.

Chapter 6

1. Martin Saarinen, *The Life Cycle of a Congregation* (Washington, D.C.: The Alban Institute, 1986). My diagram is adapted from the diagram on page 5.

2. Ibid., 2-4.

3. Ibid., 22-23.

4. Ibid., 20.

5. Ibid., 22-23.

6. Roy M. Oswald and Speed B. Leas, *The Inviting Church* (Washington, D.C.: The Alban Institute, 1987), 72-73.

7. Oswald and Leas, 75.

8. Lyle Schaller, *Assimilating New Members* (Nashville: Abingdon, 1978), 51ff.

9. Gene and Nancy Preston, "A Friendly Church Is Hard to Find," *Christian Century,* January 30, 1991, 102-3.

10. Oswald, 29.

Chapter 7

1. Arthur Weiser, *The Psalms* (Philadelphia: The Westminster Press,

1962), 401-11.

2. Ibid.

3. Manfred Brauch, *Dynamics of Renewal: A Biblical Study* (Valley Forge: American Baptist Churches, 1992), 4.

4. Ibid., 4.

5. Saarinen, 23.

6. R. C. Dentan, "Heart," *The Interpreter's Dictionary of the Bible* (New York: Abingdon Press, 1962), 550.

7. Weiser, 406.

8. David S. Young, *James: Faith in Action* (Elgin: Brethren Press, 1992), 11-21.

9. For a practical way of centering prayer, see sources such as M. Basil Pennington, *The Gospel's Invitation to Deeper Prayer* (New York: Doubleday, 1990) and Thomas Kelly, *A Testament of Devotion* (New York: Harper & Brothers, 1941).

10. Weiser, 407-8.

11. "Assimilating New Members: The Workshop Videotapes," featuring Roy M. Oswald (Washington, D.C.: The Alban Institute, 1991).

12. Available from Church Development Resources, 2850 Kalamazoo Ave., SE, Grand Rapids, MI 49560.

13. *Discover Your Gifts,* 22-47.

Chapter 8

1. See the video "Lay Ministry: Nobody Gets Off the Hook" with Bill Turpie. It explores how Christians are called to full-time ministry in the world by telling of three persons whose stories are not about being successful but about being faithful. Contact National Ministries, American Baptist Churches in the U.S.A., P.0. Box 851, Valley Forge 19482-0851. See also the video "You Can't Do That in Church" with Ezra Earl Jones, General Secretary of the United Methodist Board of Discipleship of the United Methodist Church. Through a unique approach he tells how the primary task of congregations is in reaching out and receiving persons as they are, relating them to God and one another, and developing and equipping them to go out into their communities in ministry. Contact ECU Film Library, United Methodist Church, 810 Twelfth Ave. S., Nashville, TN 37203 (1-800-251-4091).

2. Such resources could include E. Herman, *Creative Prayer,* a devotional classic available from Forward Movement Publications, 412 Sycamore St., Cincinatti, OH 45202; Douglas Steere, *Prayer in the Contemporary World* (Wallingford: Pendle Hill Publications, 1990); *Weavings,* a journal of the Christian spiritual life by the Upper Room, 1908 Grand Ave,, P.O. Box 189, Nashville, TN 37202; Henri Nouwen, *With Open Hands* (New York: Random House, 1972).

3. Church of the Brethren, General Offices, 1451 Dundee Ave., Elgin IL 60120. The American Baptist Church is engaged in Renewal 2000, a denominational emphasis for each church to look at renewal. For a variety of resources, consultations, and training events, contact the Division of Evan-

gelistic and New Church Ministries, P.O. Box 851, Valley Forge, PA 19482-0851.

4. David S. Young, "Sunday Schools that Transform," *Builder* (February 1989), 15.

5. For an excellent exposition of the quality of congregational life not being a wish dream but a "divine reality," see Dietrich Bonhoeffer, *Life Together,* trans. John Doberstein (New York: Harper and Row, 1954), 26. Good for a congregational study, as it explores the quality of Christian life in the community of faith.

6. For an interesting comparison of commitments of individuals to a congregation that results in two types of congregation styles, see Lyle Schaller, *The Decision-Makers: How to Improve the Quality of Decision-Making in the Churches* (New York: Abingdon Press, 1974), 58-59.

7. Roy M. Oswald with Jackie McMakin, *How to Prevent Lay Leader Burnout* (Washington, D.C.: The Alban Institute, Inc., 1984), 30, 37.

8. Ibid., 31.

9. Ibid., 32-33.

10. Jean Vanier, *Reflections on Christian Community* (Richmond Hill, Ontario: Daybreak Publications, 1977).

11. Ibid., 1-2.

12. Henri Nouwen, *Life of the Beloved: Spiritual Living in a Secular World* (New York: Crossroad Publishing Co., 1992).

13. Merrill Abbey, *Communication in Pulpit and Parish* (Philadelphia: The Westminster Press, 1973), 153ff.

14. Ibid., 154-58.

15. Contents from Master Class in Preaching with Dr. James Forbes, Auburn Theological Seminary on the campus of Union Theological Seminary, New York, 1984. See also James Forbes, *The Holy Spirit and Preaching* (Nashville: Abingdon Press, 1989).

16. Mitchell Dahood, S.J., trans., *The Anchor Bible,* Psalms II, 51-100 (Garden City: Doubleday & Co., 1968), 2.

17. D. Harvey, "Joy," *The Interpreter's Dictionary of the Bible*, Vol. II (New York: Abingdon Press, 1962), 1000.

18. Victor Furnish, trans., *The Anchor Bible,* II Corinthians (New York: Doubleday & Co.,1984), 401-2.

19. Herbert May and Bruce Metzger, ed., *Oxford Annotated Bible* (New York: Oxford University Press, 1962), 1302.

20. William Barclay, trans., *The Letters of John and Jude* (Philadelphia: The Westminster Press, 1960), 24-25.

Bibliography

Abbey, Merrill. *Communication in Pulpit and Parish.* Philadelphia: The Westminster Press, 1973.

"Assimilating New Members." Workshop videotapes featuring Roy Oswald. Washington, D.C.: The Alban Institute, 1991.

Barclay, William. *The Daily Study Bible Series: The Letters of John and Jude.* Philadelphia: The Westminster Press, 1960.

Bolles, Richard. *What Color Is Your Parachute?* Berkeley: Ten Speed Press, 1972.

Brauch, Manfred. *Dynamics of Renewal: A Biblical Study.* Valley Forge: American Baptist Churches, 1992.

Dentan, R. C. "Heart." *The Interpreter's Dictionary of the Bible.* 4 Vols. New York: Abingdon Press, 1962.

Dahood, Mitchell. The Anchor Bible: Psalms II. Garden City: Doubleday & Co., 1968.

Discover Your Gifts. Grand Rapids: Church Development Resources, 1983.

Forbes, James. *The Holy Spirit and Preaching.* Nashville: Abingdon, 1989.

Forbes, James. Master Class in Preaching, Auburn Theological Seminary on the campus of Union Theological Seminary, New York, 1984.

Furnish, Victor. Trans. notes, introduction, and commentary. *The Anchor Bible.* II Corinthians. New York: Doubleday & Co. 1984.

German, Richard and Peter Arnold. *Job and Career Building.* New York: Harper and Row, 1980.

Greenleaf, Robert, *The Servant as Leader.* Cambridge: Center for Applied Studies, 1973.

Harvey, D. "Joy." *The Interpreter's Dictionary of the Bible.* New York: Abingdon Press, 1962.

Hesse, Hermann. *The Journey to the East.* New York: The Noonday Press, 1956.

Johnson, Douglas. *The Care and Feeding of Volunteers.* Nashville: Abingdon, 1987.

Kittel, Gerhard, gen. ed. *Theological Dictionary of the New Testament.* Translated and edited by Geoffrey W Bromiley. 8 Vols. Grand Rapids: William B. Eerdmanns Publishing Co., 1964-1972.

Lawrie, J. W. "Leadership and Magical Thinking." *Personnel Journal.* September 1970.

Mager, Roger. *Preparing Instructional Objectives.* Belmont: Lear Siegler, Inc., 1962.

Manson, T. W. *Ministry and Priesthood, Christ's and Ours.* Richmond: John Knox Press, n.d.

May, Herbert and Bruce Metzger, eds. *Oxford Annotated Bible.* New York: Oxford University Press, 1962.

Moss, James. *People Spots.* Harrisburg: E. Pa. Conference, Churches of God, 1988.

Nouwen, Henri. *Life of the Beloved: Spiritual Living in a Secular World.* New York: Crossroad Publishing Co., 1992.

Nouwen, Henri. Personal correspondence with Henri Nouwen on the connection between servanthood and deep prayer, October 29, 1986.

Oswald, Roy, with Jackie McMakin. *How to Prevent Lay Leader Burnout.* Washington: The Alban Institute, 1984.

Oswald, Roy, and Speed Leas. *The Inviting Church.* Washington: The Alban Institute, 1987.

Parish Consultation Skills Training. Mid-Atlantic District Church of the Brethren, New Windsor, Maryland. January 26-28, 1972.

Preston, Gene and Nancy. "A Friendly Church Is Hard to Find." *Christian Century.* January 1991.

Rothauge, Arlin. *Sizing Up a Congregation for New Member Ministry.* New York: The Episcopal Church Center, n.d.

Saarinen, Martin. *The Life Cycle of the Congregation.* Washington: The Alban Institute, 1986.

Schaller, Lyle. *Assimilating New Members.* Nashville: Abingdon Press, 1987.

Schaller, Lyle. *The Decision Makers: How to Improve the Quality of Decision Making in the Churches.* New York: Abingdon Press, 1974.

Vanier, Jean. *Reflections on Christian Community.* Richmond Hill, Ontario: Daybreak Publications, 1977.

Weiser, Arthur. *The Psalms.* Philadelphia: The Westminster Press, 1962.

Young, David S. *How the Pastor Can Help Motivate and Supervise Renewal in the Local Congregation.* Unpublished D.Min. Thesis, Bethany Theological Seminary, 1976.

Young, David S. *James: Faith in Action.* Elgin: The Brethren Press, 1992.

Young, David S. "Marks of Ministry." *Messenger.* May 1987.

Young, David S. "Sunday Schools that Transform." *Builder.* February 1989.

Additional Places to Turn

For Consulting, Resourcing, and Training

The American Baptist Church, Division of Evangelistic and New Church Ministries, P.O. Box 851, Valley Forge, PA 19482-0851.

The Alban Institute, 4550 Montgomery Ave., Suite 433 North, Bethesda, MD 20814-3341.

The Andrew Center, 1451 Dundee Ave., Elgin, IL 60120 (1-800-774-3360).

For Readings on Church Renewal

Buttry, Daniel. *Bring Your Church Back to Life.* Valley Forge: Judson Press, 1988.

Carroll, Jackson, Carl Dudley, and William McKinney. *Handbook for Congregational Studies.* Nashville: Abingdon Press, 1986.

McIntosh, Duncan, and Richard Rusbuldt, *Planning Growth in Your Church.* Valley Forge: Judson Press, 1983.

Mead, Loren. *The Once and Future Church: Reinventing the Congregation for a New Mission Frontier.* Washington, D.C.: The Alban Institute, 1991.

Moss, James. *People Spots.* Harrisburg, E. Pa. Conference, Churches of God, 1984.

Schaller, Lyle. *Assimilating New Members.* Nashville: Abingdon Press, 1978.

For Implementing Servant Leadership

Resources from the Robert Greenleaf Center for Servant Leadership, 1100 W. 42d St., Suite 321, Indianapolis, IN 46208.

O'Connor, Elizabeth . *Servant Leaders, Servant Structures.* Washington, D.C.: The Servant Leadership School, 1991. Order from the Servant Leadership School, 1640 Columbia Rd., NW, Washington, D.C. 20009.

For Writings on the Spiritual Life

Vanier, Jean. "Welcoming Jesus in the Poor." Richmond Hill, Ontario: Daybreak Publications, 1987. See also Jean Vanier, "Reflections on Christian Community." Richmond Hill, Ontario: Daybreak Publications, 1977. These monographs are available from Daybreak Publications, 11339 Yonge St., Richmond Hill, Ontario L4C 4X7.

Weavings: A Journal of the Christian Spiritual Life, 1908 Grand Ave., P.O. Box 851, Nashville, TN 37202-9890.